The Pecan Man

Cassie Dandridge Selleck

For Nicholas

Lighter of candles and finder of lost things

Acknowledgements

Over the years, I have worked on this story with the invaluable help of the Gainesville Poets and Writers group. It would be impossible to name them all, but special thanks to the core members Charlotte, Christy, Gen, Dorothy, Eldon, Art, Mary, Stephanie, Donald, Jani and many others who poured their time and energy into this work, offering honest critique and tremendous encouragement over the years. To my dear friends Teresa Renfrow Masters, Cheryl Pulliam, Rick Sgabellone, Perky Granger and the wonderful women of the Mayo Woman's Club, I thank you for your warm friendship, constant support and occasional kick in the behind. It has been a blessing to have people who believe in me and push me to sit down and write.

To my daughters Patti, Katie and Emily: You have been a constant source of inspiration and encouragement and I am so proud of the beautiful young women you have become.

To my parents, Patty and Frank Dandridge: Thank you for raising us in a home where all who entered were literally welcomed with open arms. You taught us the meaning of love and acceptance and I will always be grateful for that. I love you dearly.

To my siblings Petey, Bubba and Pat, step-daughter Kimie and countless cousins, nieces, nephews, and my beloved grandbabies, I love you all so much.

To my dear friend Julie Williams Sanon: You are my sister as if we were born of the same blood. Thank you for teaching me by example to love as Jesus loved.

And last as always, but first in my heart – my sweet, sweet husband: I will love you always.

One

In the summer of 1976, the year of our Bicentennial, preparations for the Fourth of July were in full force. Flags hung from the eaves of every house along this stretch of Main Street. The neighborhood women were even busier than usual. I watched them come and go from a rocking chair on my own front porch.

Every now and then a slight breeze moved the heavy, humid air and, if there was no traffic going by, I could hear the flags rustling along the row. I sat with a piece of cardboard in one hand and a glass of sweet tea in the other. The ice always melted before I emptied the glass. I used the cardboard to augment the gentle blowing of the ceiling fan, which I was sure put out more heat than cool with its low purring motor constantly going. I kept it on though. I liked the sound.

Back then, the streets of our small Florida town were not unlike the streets of Andy Taylor's Mayberry, or Atticus Finch's Maycomb. We even have a similar name, Mayville. I always like to say, "That May sure got around, now didn't she?"

There's no one here to laugh at my jokes anymore. I used to have a maid who came every day. Blanche was black as pitch and twice as heavy. I asked her once how she got her name, seeing as how Blanche is French for white and she wasn't even close. She said she was born as light-skinned as me and that her daddy had left soon afterwards saying no baby of his could be that pale.

Her mama waited a couple of days before naming her. Just held her and rocked her and sang her own tears dry. Seems she was more than positive she had never lain down with another man since the day she was born and she felt certain he would believe her and come home. When he didn't, she carried the baby in her arms all the way to the public library just off Main Street. Libraries back then wouldn't check out books to Negroes, so she found a book of baby names and sat right down on the floor. Nestling her sleeping infant between her crossed legs, she started on the A's. When she got to Blanche and saw what it meant, she reckoned it was as fitting and pretty a name as she had ever seen, so Blanche it was.

Had her daddy stuck around a bit, he'd have seen his baby girl turn darker and darker as the months rolled by. Blanche once told me she figured he was the one who lost out, not her, and I thought that was a right healthy way to look at it.

Blanche worked for me through birth and death, joy and sorrow, and Lord knows we had a lot of sorrow in all the time we spent under this roof. Most people figured she was crazy to put up with me all those years, but Blanche and I had an understanding. It was a vow we made those long years ago. Neither of us spoke of it afterwards, but it hung between us like a spider web, fragile and easy to break, but danged hard to get shed of once the threads took hold.

It's been a quarter of a century since fate sealed the two of us together. Blanche got fatter, but never looked a day older than she did back then. I, on the other hand, have managed to get thinner and more fragile, if that's possible. I'm eighty-two years old. I was fifty-seven then, and recently widowed. I'd tell you about my husband, Walter, but he doesn't really play a part in this story so I reckon there's not much point. Funny, I don't remember what color Walter's eyes were. I'll chalk that up to what age does to an already feeble mind. But I remember every single detail about what happened with the Pecan Man.

Though mostly vacant these days, the buildings on Main Street once housed dress shops and jewelry stores with diamonds and gemstones glistening on oceans of blue velvet in the front windows. Ezell's Department store survived the arrival of J.C. Penney, with its shiny tile floors and ornate marble staircase, but they went to mostly rugged men's wear for years afterward. Penney's could never compete with the smell of denim and leather and the creak of wooden floors when it came to the male populace.

In 1976, the bank was building its new home out on the highway and their old four-story relic downtown was sold to a company that provided counseling and other services to alcoholics, drug addicts and the like. They called it Lifeways, but that was just a euphemism for nuthouse and most of the residents weren't going to stand for that kind of element in our neighborhood.

Dovey Kincaid got up a petition to keep them out and we all signed it, but we lost in the end. Frank Perley was head of the city commission and he made sure his wife's cousin's company got in. After that our neighborhood went downhill fast. People moved out by the truckload and practically gave their family homes away.

It's still a beautiful, if somewhat ragged, neighborhood and I do what I can to keep my own house looking stately and neat. Our streets are lined with pecan trees so large that two men could wrap their arms around their trunks and only barely touch fingertips. The trees used to look majestic, but now they just look tired. Their limbs droop miserably and the Spanish moss that once served as regal attire now hangs limp and shaggy like the beards of the homeless old men who pass by daily on their way downtown.

Several blocks from there, the opposite direction of my neighborhood, is what we call *colored town*. Oh, I know it's not right to call it that these days, but that was what we called it then and I'm too old to relearn the etiquette I had drilled into my head from the time I could hold a spoon.

Blanche raised five children of her own there, plus the two grandchildren she took in when her youngest daughter ran off with a drug dealer. She might have been mad at that child if she hadn't known what she did about the whole situation. As it was, Blanche couldn't find it in her heart to blame her daughter for any of the bad choices she made, considering the role she played in this story.

The events of that year were the real driving force behind the mass exodus from the neighborhood. It was the year of the Pecan Man. None of us knew how much impact one skinny old colored man could have in our lives, but we found out soon enough.

There is a wooded area not far from downtown that has sat neglected for as long as I can remember, although it was not nearly so grown over with weeds when I was a child and played there. It is widely known now to shelter several homeless men, one of whom is blatantly crazy and should be an inpatient, if you ask me.

Back then, only one man was known to inhabit the place and that was the Pecan Man. Whoever first gave the man the name pronounced it *Pee-can* and it stuck.

The Pecan Man took up residence there in the summer of 1975, but it took a while before anyone ever figured out he actually lived there. Maybe it was his gaunt frame or the ghostly way he just seemed to appear from those woods riding a bicycle as old as he was and every bit as thin and rumpled. Whatever it was about him that struck people as frightful, it didn't take long before parents took to calling their children in whenever he appeared.

They called him the Pecan Man because he always had a sack full of pecans tied to the handlebars of his rickety old bike. Turns out he got most of his sustenance from the nuts of those prolific trees. He'd stop all along his route to who-knows-where, picking up any pecans that had rolled onto the sidewalk or street, but leaving alone any that so much as touched the yard of the tree's owner. This was the widely accepted rule and I never saw anyone break it, not even the children, and I've spent many an hour on this porch watching.

The neighborhood children made up a song that they sang as they jumped rope in their yards. I heard it enough times to know it by heart and I still wake up some nights in a cold sweat with the rhyme pounding over and over in my head.

> *Mama call the po-lice*
> *Catch him if you can*
> *Everybody scared of the Pecan Man*

Then they'd launch into a list as long as they could make it by filling in the names of every man, woman and child they knew. The winner was the one who called out the most names without missing a jump.

> *David scared of the Pecan Man*
> *Jimbo scared of the Pecan Man*
> *Mary Beth scared of the Pecan Man*
> *Rheda Gail scared of the Pecan Man*
> *Miss Abernathy scared of the Pecan Man*

and so on.

Two

When you're as old as I am, it takes a while to make a point. The Pecan Man had a name—Eldred Mims. I called him Eddie. The people of Mayville didn't know his name at all, until he was arrested and charged with the murder of a sixteen year old boy named Skipper Kornegay.

Now, twenty-five years later, his name has made the papers again. I suppose it is noteworthy news that Eldred Mims died in prison of old age. His sentence was twenty-five years to life. I guess it worked out on both counts.

I feel pretty certain that most townspeople would just as soon forget the man, but now that I'm the only one left who even knows the whole truth, I think it's time I told it.

In the spring of 1976, the Pecan Man began mowing my lawn. For two weeks I watched him ride that rickety old bike out of the woods dragging an equally pathetic lawn mower behind him. He wouldn't return until late afternoon, his ragged shirt plastered to his gaunt body by wind and sweat. I figured he'd found a few yards to mow outside of our neighborhood, since no one near us would hire him. This was before the murder, mind you, when people just *thought* he was dangerous because he was homeless and black. *After* the murder they were certain of it. I just thought he looked hungry and I was willing to take a risk.

On the third Monday that I watched him strike out for parts unknown, I flagged him down with a whistle my Mama taught me years ago. It's a pretty darn good whistle, too. It startled him enough to make him bring his bike to a shaky halt at my driveway. I waved him up to the porch. He left the mower and pushed the bike as far as the stoop.

"Mawnin', Ma'am."

Eldred Mims had an unusual voice, high-pitched and squeaky, and each word was punctuated by the smacking noise made when his toothless gums made contact. It was like they were made of suction cups. The sound was distracting at first, but you got used to it easy enough.

I used to joke to Blanche that I couldn't understand why the neighbors were so afraid of the man.

"One thing was certain," I'd tell her, "He may gum you to death, but he sure ain't gonna bite."

Where was I now? Oh, yes, Eldred Mims stood in front of me; beat up old cap in hand.

"Mighty fine day, isn't it?" I asked him with a wave of my fan.

"Yes'm," he smacked out his reply. "Look like it go'n be fine, 'jes fine."

"Care for a glass of tea?"

He looked taken aback by my question, as if it were the last one on earth he expected me to ask. Then he shuffled his feet, rubbed his neck with the hand that held his limp cap and mumbled something I couldn't understand.

"Speak up, man!" I complained. "I can't hear worth a hoot."

"I said, No'm, tha's okay, but I thank you for axin'. I sho' nuff do."

"Hot as it is out here, you don't want tea? What's the matter with you that you can't accept my hospitality?"

Now, I knew doggone good and well he was trying to be polite by not accepting, but I was pretty sure it had been a while since he'd had a glass of cold sweet tea and, quite frankly, he looked like he could use some. I pressed on.

"Blanche!" I hollered over my shoulder, throwing my voice in the general direction of the door.

Blanche's wide body appeared in the doorway a moment later. I always got a kick out of watching her materialize at that screen door as if by magic. Of course, there wasn't any magic to it. It was just that you couldn't see her until she got right up to the screen and the outside light hit her white uniform.

"Blanche, we have a visitor here. Could you bring this gentleman a glass of tea?"

She answered by stepping out of the door and reaching for my glass.

"I'll get you some more while I'm at it." And she disappeared the same way she came.

"I'm Ora Lee Beckworth," I said with a far less intimidating tone.

"Pleased to meet you, Ma'am," was his shaky reply.

"You got a name?"

"I reckon I do, but mos' folks jus' call me the Pecan Man."

"I knew that much," I said, "but, I'd rather call you your given name, if you have one."

"Eldred, Ma'am."

I realize now that he must have said "Eldred Mims" and not "Eldred, Ma'am" like I thought, but that's the way I heard it at the time.

"What'd your mama call you?" I asked.

He grinned then, displaying an engaging smile despite the missing teeth. "She call't me Eddie."

"Eddie it is, then," I said and returned his smile.

Blanche reappeared with the tea just as I persuaded him to park his bike and sit on the edge of the stoop. He mumbled a *thanks* and took the glass from her, holding it tightly in his lap like he was afraid he might break it.

"So, you mow lawns for a living?" I asked.

"Yes'm, I do."

"Interested in doing mine?"

"Yes'm, I reckon I am."

"Okay, good. This is what I need. Every Wednesday morning, I need my front and back lawn mowed. Every Saturday, I need my flowerbeds weeded and hedges trimmed as necessary. Can you handle that for me, and how much do you charge?"

"I can do that for ya, Miz Beckworth. Won't cost ya' but five dollars a week, I figure."

"Five dollars a week!" I let my indignation set in before I continued. "Why, that's highway robbery! And I'll have you know, I am *not* a thief!"

He looked at me, confused and slightly horrified, but his eyes lit up when he realized what I meant.

"I'll pay you ten dollars and not a penny less."

He grinned again. "Yes'm, that'll be fine. It sho' will be fine."

"A day," I added, pleased with his reaction and even more pleased with myself for causing it.

His face fell.

"No'm," he said, "that'd be too much. I can't take ten dollars a day jus' for mowin' this here little bitty lawn and pullin' some puny weeds out da' garden."

I realized I'd pushed it too far and, though I thought the job well worth my offer, I backed down without taking offense at his unintentional disparagement of my garden.

"Fine," I said, "but lunch and all the tea you can drink come with the job both days. And, if I were you, I wouldn't turn down one of

Blanche's sandwiches or she'll be downright offended."

"I'll 'member that. I sho' will."

After he left that day, Blanche appeared at the screen door with a pot of beans in one hand and two colanders in the other. We sat in companionable silence listening to the low whirring of the fan and the rhythmic creaking of our rockers keeping time for the soft percussive pops of the beans we snapped. When we'd finished all she'd brought out, she set her colander in the crook of her arm and sat gently rocking as if she held a sleeping baby and not a pot of beans. Finally, she stood up and gathered all she'd brought out. She didn't look at me when she spoke. She looked out across the front lawn.

"That man is old and homeless, but he ain't stupid, Miz Beckworth. Don't be hurtin' his pride more than he can take, you hear me?"

I didn't answer, but she knew I heard.

Eddie showed up on time every single day he worked for me. I never saw him with a watch, but he always seemed to know what time it was. He would start mowing promptly at 10:00 a.m. and finish just before noon. He would never join me on the porch, but ate on the same side of the stoop without fail.

We didn't talk much, although Lord knows I tried to get information from that raggedy old man. I think it was the not knowing that made people nervous. Several of my neighbors made their disappointment in my choice of employees readily apparent, but I ignored most of their complaints. That is, until Dovey Kincaid dropped by with a lemon chess pie and a bucketful of advice.

I've known Dovey since she was a newlywed and moved into the house across the street. I'm only fifteen years her elder, but by then she was treating me like I was old and feebleminded.

"Hey, Miss Beckworth!"

Southerners *always* call their elders Mr. or Miss Whatever. Doesn't matter if you're married or not; the only thing that changes with familiarity is whether they call you by your first or your last name.

Anyway, Dovey never called me Miss Ora Lee. I never liked her enough to let her get familiar. Truth be known, callin' me Miss Beckworth was her way of saying she didn't want to be familiar in the first place, but that was fine with me. Southerners are mostly happy to give tit for tat.

Dovey didn't wait to be invited to sit down. She put the pie down on the table beside me and settled her big ol' square behind into one of my rockers.

"Beautiful day, ain't it, Miss Beckworth?"

"It started out that way." I could barely disguise my contempt. Dovey Kincaid hasn't visited me one time in her life to be social. I could tell right off she was on a mission.

"It sure did, Miss Beckworth. It really did." She sighed like she'd just had a bite of heaven and settled herself into the rocker.

"What brings you all the way across the street, Dovey?"

"Well, I was just bakin' a few pies for the Woman's Club bake sale and I looked out and saw you sittin' here and I thought to myself, 'Now, Dovey Kincaid! Here you are bakin' pies for charity, and there sits your very own neighbor over there all by herself!' So, I whipped off my apron, picked up a lemon chess pie and headed right on over." She smoothed her skirt with both hands, then clasped them together like she was saying a prayer and dropped them into her lap. Then, as if she had forgotten her manners, leaned forward, cocked her head to the side and aimed her best debutante smile right in my direction.

I grinned back, but not in the name of being mannerly.

"Is that so, Dovey?" I chuckled. "Well, that is just as charitable a thing as I can imagine. I'll make sure Blanche takes it home with her tonight."

I asked a mental prayer of forgiveness for insulting Blanche that way, but I just couldn't help myself.

"Oh! Well, of course, Miss Beckworth," she sputtered as tat collided solidly with tit (if you'll pardon the expression). "But, I do hope you'll try a little bite yourself before you do. I worked awful hard on that pie for you not to at least get a taste of it."

"I appreciate the thought, but I'm afraid it might be a little sour for me. Lemon gives me gas."

Judging by her expression of horror, she no doubt wanted me to think I had offended her gentility, but she forgets the fact that sound carries a long way when windows are open. She may not have lost her virginity on her wedding night, but Lord knows she lost any discretion she might have had.

"What do you really want, Dovey?" I asked as she composed herself.

"Well, I did want to ask you about that awful old man you've hired to mow your lawn. Now, I know it's none of my business, but do you think it's a good idea to have him in this neighborhood all the time? Honestly, Miss Beckworth, we don't know a thing about this man and you've got him over here plunderin' through everything."

"Plundering? He's weeding my garden! How do you get plundering out of a little yard work?"

"Well, you know what I mean. He's just getting mighty familiar with your property. It isn't right, Miss Beckworth! The other day, I saw him rummaging through your garage when your back was turned."

"I sent him to look for some slug pellets, Dovey. He's trying to get my flowerbeds back in order, for crying out loud."

"Well, still—I don't think it's good for him to be around all the time. It's bad enough that we're three blocks from the loony bin. Now folks ridin' through will be thinking the neighborhood's gone colored all the sudden. And besides, it just isn't safe."

"Oh, for heaven's sake! That man couldn't hurt a fly if he wanted to. He's seventy years old if he's a day." (I was ten years off on that, but I didn't know it at the time.)

"Maybe so, but he's got a dangerous look to him and I don't like it. And he's fit enough to haul that mower around everywhere he goes. That says to me that he's fit enough to do whatever harm he has a mind to."

"Well, it says to me he's hungry, Dovey, and if you had a charitable bone in your body, you'd be baking a pie for *him*. Now, you can take that pie of yours and waddle your fat butt on home. No one here needs your kind of charity."

Don't you know, she scooped that pie up and was back inside her front door before the rocker she vacated came to a rest.

Three

Summer came and went without much excitement. Eldred Mims became a fixture in the neighborhood. Mothers stopped calling their children inside the moment they saw him and life returned to normal, as we knew it anyway.

Just about the time we finally smelled fall in the air the family grocery store downtown succumbed to the rise of the supermarket. Neither Blanche nor I were able to walk the mile or so it now took to get groceries, so I started taking a cab to the Winn Dixie store. The wide variety of choices was overwhelming at first and it often took over two hours to finish my marketing. Blanche pitched a fit the first time I did that.

"Law, Miss Ora, you 'bout scared me to death!"

Blanche could be dramatic when she had a mind to be.

"Quit fussing and help me unpack this stuff."

I was too tired to account for my whereabouts, dull as the story might be.

"You couldn'ta been at the Winn Dixie all this time! Why didn't you tell me you was go'n go somewheres else?"

"Well, I was and I didn't, Blanche. It took me all this long to get through that blasted store. I've never seen so much food in all my life. I don't know why Bobby Milstead had to go and close the Thriftway downtown."

"They like to blame it on those big ol' stores, Miss Ora, but I know for a fact it's 'cause Mr. Bobby's son wadn't no account. Mr. Bobby been wantin' to retire for ten years now and he was just waitin' for Bobby, Jr. to grow up and take an interest.

"My Marcus stocked shelves down there for three years. He wanted to buy that ol' store, but Mr. Bobby wouldn't have none of that. He said he'd rather close it down than to have somebody else run it into the ground. That's why Marcus up and join't the Army."

"My Lord, Blanche, you never said a word about that."

"Wasn't much to say," she said and shrugged. "Marcus, couldn't have bought it anyway."

"Too much?" I asked.

Blanche looked at me like I had two heads.

"Yeah, Miz Ora, that's it," she said, "It cost too much."

Her sarcasm wasn't lost on me, but I was too exhausted to pursue it further. I poured a glass of tea and headed for my porch, leaving Blanche to deal with the groceries.

Within a month or two, I had my shopping excursions down to two hours every other week. I grew to appreciate the fact that I could get pantyhose AND medicine in the same store where I bought chicken legs. I wondered why I hadn't tried this before. Blanche reminded me about old dogs and new tricks when I said that out loud. Sometimes I wonder why I kept her around all those years.

September 24th. I'll remember that date for as long as I live. That was the day that really set this thing into motion.

I came home from the Winn Dixie to find Blanche sitting in my recliner, clutching her youngest child Grace to her chest. The child was sleeping, but I could see muddy streaks of tears that had dried on her face. Blanche's face was still wet, though the only sound that came from her mouth was the song she was singing soft and low to her baby girl.

"What in the world..." My voice trailed off as I dropped the sacks I carried to the floor. "Blanche, what has happened?"

I heard someone clear his throat behind me and turned to see the cab driver with an armload of groceries.

"Oh...yes...set them down here. Are there any more?"

He nodded as he put the grocery bags on the seat of the hall tree next to the door. Blanche still had not looked up or altered her low singing. I followed the cab driver out, paid what I owed and took the last of the groceries from his arms. I tottered back into the house and set the paper bags on the dining room table.

Blanche still hadn't responded to my question. She just kept up her soft crooning while a tiny river of tears ran down her cheeks. I knelt beside the chair and quietly laid both my hands on her arm.

"Blanche. What is it? Tell me what happened."

She didn't respond, but began to whimper softly.

"Blanche, it's all right now. It's all right."

"It ain't all right, Miss Ora. It ain't all right and it ain't never *gonna* be all right."

Grace stirred in her mama's arms and Blanche held her tighter and rocked harder in the chair.

"What's not all right, Blanche? What happened? Lord, please tell me what happened."

But Blanche did not respond. She closed her eyes and rocked her child.

I suddenly felt faint. In all the time Blanche had worked for me I had never seen her cry. I kicked off my shoes and went to the kitchen. I could still hear Blanche's rhythmic rocking and the soft, sad tune she hummed to her baby girl.

A pitcher of tea and two glasses were already out on the counter. Blanche had apparently been anticipating my return. I cracked a tray of ice and winced as the ice cubes hit the insides of the glasses.

Too loud, I thought.

The cubes cracked again as I poured the warm tea over them. I took a long drink from one of the glasses and took the other to Blanche. Her shoulders pulsed up and down as if she were bouncing Grace like an infant with colic, but as I approached I saw that the shaking was caused by the deep, silent sobs Blanche was trying to control. I set the tea down on the lamp table beside the chair, then leaned over and reached for the child.

"Let me have her, Blanche."

I'd never heard my own voice sound like that—low, firm and commanding. Blanche responded by rolling Grace even tighter to her bosom.

"Give her to me, Blanche."

"She too heavy for you, Miss Ora. Jes' let me hol' her here a while. Then I'll get up and put those groceries away."

"For crying out loud, Blanche. I don't give a rat's ass about the groceries! The child's exhausted. I'm going to put her to bed, and then you are going to tell me what happened so we can figure out what to do about it."

"Ain't nothin' we can do about it. Nothin' a'tall."

I reached down again and lifted Grace into my arms. Blanche didn't try to stop me this time. I was surprised at how tiny the child felt, not heavy at all. I'd never held her before.

Grace took a shuddering breath, but stayed asleep as I carried her down the hall to the guest bedroom. Sunlight streamed through the window on the west wall and fell on the child's face as I bent to pull back the covers. I stopped and stared at her for a moment.

I put her in bed and removed her patent leather shoes and ruffled socks. I saw the streak of blood then, already turning brown and blending into the black scuffs of dirt and grass stains on the once white cotton. Gracie's skin was dark like her mama's, and it took a moment to realize that her legs were covered in the same dirt and scuffs and, though I could see no open wounds on her body, blood. It lay in streaks down the insides of her thin, baby legs. I covered them then, willing myself not to see what I was seeing. My soft white sheets and pink chenille spread had never suppressed such offense and I would never look at them again without remembering.

I drew the shades and stopped at the door to look back at the sleeping child. I hadn't felt angry until that moment, only concern and confusion. But, as I stood there watching Blanche's precious child sleep, fury churned in my stomach and spread its heat through my chest and down my arms. I didn't feel my fingernails cut into the palms of my hands as I clenched and unclenched my fists, but I saw the marks later and knew exactly when it happened.

I closed the door and went back down the hall toward the living room. Blanche was carrying the last sacks of groceries to the kitchen. I didn't say a word. What could I possibly have said? I did the same thing Blanche did. I tried to force normalcy back into our world. I put the canned goods into the pantry while Blanche worked on the cold food. She closed the refrigerator door just as I came out of the pantry. Our eyes met and we froze.

Then, as I stood there trying and failing to find words of comfort or wisdom or anything that wouldn't be dismally inadequate, I watched Blanche collapse into herself. It began with her forehead, then her eyes and mouth. Her hands flew up to cover her face, but the rest of her went down, down, down. I reached for her, but there was no way to hold her up. My rage was no match for her sorrow and we went down together.

I don't know how long we stayed there. Long enough for Blanche's anguished sobs to dissipate. Long enough for the room to grow dark with the setting of the sun. Long enough for Blanche's oldest daughter to worry about her mother not being home to fix supper.

Four

The harsh jangling of the telephone brought us both to our feet. Blanche reached the phone in the hallway first, but I took it from her before she could speak.

"Hello?" My voice cracked a little.

"Miz Beckworth?" It was Patrice.

"Hey, Sugar. You worried about your mama? I shoulda called you a long time ago and I just forgot." I forced cheer into my voice and rushed on before she could respond. "Blanche isn't feeling too well, honey. I'm just gonna put her in the guest room and have her stay the night. You're all right there, aren't you? Can you get the others fed okay? How old are you now? Sixteen, isn't it?"

"Yes'm, I'll be seventeen next month. And we done had supper, but ... is Mama okay?"

"She's just feelin' a little poorly, but she'll be fine. I think she ate something that didn't agree with her."

"Is Grace all right there, too? Do you want me to come get her?"

"No, that's okay. She's already asleep, so she'll stay here, too."

"I didn't mean for her to stay the whole day over there. She drew Mama a picture at school and was just set on takin' it straight to her. I thought Mama'd send her right on back home and I've kinda been worried about her. I hope she hasn't been botherin' you."

"Lord, child, Grace is no bother. Don't you worry a bit. Your mama will call you tomorrow mornin' to check on y'all, okay?"

"I don't know, Miz Ora. I really think I oughta talk to Mama about it. Can she come to the phone?"

"Well," I hesitated, "not right this minute, but I can have her call you in a little bit if it's not too urgent." Blanche reached for the phone and I turned away tugging the receiver close to my ear.

"Well ... I just need to know what she wants me to do. You sure she's okay?"

I could hear the concern in her voice. It bordered on panic.

"She's fine, Patrice. I'll have her call you. Bye!"

I hung up before she could say another word. That was not one of my finer performances I'm sure, but I didn't want Blanche to talk to anyone until we'd had a chance to talk about Grace.

"I cain't leave my children overnight, Miz Ora."

"Patrice is no child, Blanche."

"I ain't never left 'em alone all night."

"I'm well aware of that," I said. "Tell you the truth, I don't know how you've done half the things you've done by yourself since Luther died."

"It's been six years now, I'm 'bout used to it. And Patrice helps me."

"What do you reckon Luther'd want you to do about this thing with Grace?"

Blanche squared her shoulders and sucked in a long breath.

"Luther woulda landed hisself in jail or worse over *'this thing'*. I never thought I'd say it, but it's prolly good he ain't here to deal with it now. The way I see it, they ain't a thing we can do that wouldn't make it worse than it already is."

"Not even calling the police?"

"Huh," Blanche grunted. "Especially not callin' the police."

"You can't believe that, Blanche."

"It ain't the same for you, Miz Ora. You jes' go'n have to trust me on this one."

Part of me knew she was dead right, but it wasn't something I wanted to admit. Not to her, anyway.

"Surely we're not still living in that kind of world..." I trailed off helplessly.

"What kind of world is that, Miz Ora? What do you think would happen to my girl—hell, to my whole family—if we went to the police with this?"

I opened my mouth to answer, but she went on.

"I'll tell you what would happen. They'd take my baby down to the hospital and they'd do their jobs, but they ain't no way she'd understand. She'd just feel like they was doin' things to her all over again. Meanwhile—"

"Blanche."

"*Meanwhile*," she nearly shouted over me, "they'd act like she couldn't hear a word they said, but she'd hear all right. She'd hear them call her a liar, even if they didn't actually use that word. And they'd make her feel dirty, 'cause *they* think she's dirty."

"Blanche, no..."

"Then the police would come askin' questions she couldn't answer. They'd do they damnedest to trip her up and it would! By the time they got done with her, she'd be doubtin' she was even my baby."

"But, I won't let that happen, Blanche. I wouldn't leave your side for a minute. I know Chief Kornegay! He would never let them get away with..."

"Chief Kornegay?! That just shows how much you *don't* know. It was Ralph Kornegay's son did this to Grace. He raped her, Miz Ora! He full out raped my baby and then he laughed in her face!"

"Oh, sweet Jesus," I moaned and turned away from her. I couldn't seem to breathe. I clutched at the front of my blouse, but my hands were trembling and the fabric slipped from my fingers. Blanche went on.

"And what if somebody did believe her? What if they did send that boy to jail for what he did? He's still in high school. Worst that would happen to him is goin' to reform school and what good would that do? What do you think would happen to Gracie at school then? They would torment her, that's what would happen."

I covered my ears with both hands and turned toward the living room.

"Okay, Blanche, okay. I understand..."

"No, you *don't* understand, Miz Ora! You don't understand at all. It wouldn't just be *hard* on her. It would never be *safe* for her again. Sooner or later, somebody would want revenge, if not before that boy got out, for sho' *after* he got out. I ain't puttin' her through it, do you hear me? I ain't!"

"I hear you, Blanche," I said. "I hear you, and Lord help me, you're probably right, but we can't just let it go. If he did this to Gracie, he'd do it to any child. We have to do something. We can't just sit here and do nothing."

Blanche put her hands on her hips and looked at me like I didn't have good sense.

"I need time to think, Miz Ora. Until then, *nothin'* is exactly what we go'n do."

I woke up early the next morning. Truth is, I barely slept at all. I peeked into the guest room at six a.m. and Blanche was sleeping soundly with her arms wrapped tightly around her youngest child.

I went to the kitchen and made a pot of coffee. I put some bacon in a cast iron skillet and pulled what was left of yesterday morning's biscuits from the bread basket on the kitchen counter. I decided to fry the biscuits in butter and scramble a few eggs once the bacon was done. I wasn't hungry. I just needed something to do.

A half hour later Blanche came down the hall looking like she'd never gone to bed. Grace was beside her, still half asleep, but Blanche had obviously cleaned her up a bit. Blanche pulled out a dining room chair and deposited the child in it. Grace promptly put her head down on the table and went back to sleep.

"How you feelin'?" I regretted the question as soon as I asked it. Blanche didn't answer.

"Want some coffee? I made some bacon and eggs, too."

"I cain't eat nothin', Miz Ora."

"Yeah, neither could I."

Blanche shuffled over to the coffee pot and poured a cup. She added milk and sugar and stood at the kitchen counter to drink her coffee. She didn't speak for several minutes.

When the silence got too heavy, I reached out and touched her arm. "Blanche?"

She didn't look up, and almost whispered when she finally spoke.

"She woke up cryin' in the middle of the night."

I thought my heart would shatter right there—just burst into a thousand tiny shards of glass and spill out between my ribs.

"Blanche..."

"I told her it was just a dream," she said. "Just a really bad dream—that it never happened at all."

"Dear, Lord..." I whispered.

"And then I prayed He'd forgive me for lyin' to my baby like that."

I offered lamely, "We're gonna get through this, Blanche."

"I reckon we are." She didn't sound convinced.

"I want you to do something for me and I won't take no for an answer." Silence.

"I want you to let Grace come here after school for a while. She can ride the bus right down to the corner and you can meet her there every day."

Blanche brought her coffee to her usual place at the table and sat heavily in her chair. She gave me a look that I took to mean she was going to object. I plowed ahead.

"Now, I know what you're going to say and I'm telling you, the child won't be any trouble. It's just for a couple of hours a day and besides, I could use the company."

Blanche coughed and stared at her cup.

"I was up all night thinking about this, Blanche. I'm here with you every day. You know my routines and I know yours. Hell, I know what you're thinking half the time, but I don't know your children."

"What're you talkin' about, Miz Ora? You know my kids."

I waved my hands at her.

"Oh, I know little things about them from the stories you tell. I know Marcus is at Fort Bragg now. I know Patrice is your studious child, your rock, the one who holds the family together when you're gone. I know the twins are boy-crazy and working on giving you gray hair and I know that Grace will never be the same again, but what I don't know is who she was before this awful thing happened to her and I don't know *why* I don't know."

I stopped and drew a deep breath. I did know why. I knew exactly why and so did Blanche. It made me sick with grief and shame.

Blanche straightened her back and sat tall in her chair. Her face was set in a way that said her decision was made. I could argue until I was blue in the face and it would not change her answer. In the brief seconds before she spoke I actually felt relieved. It was one thing to recognize myself as a fraud. It was another thing entirely to do something about it. I could console myself with the knowledge that I tried to change it, but the truth was, I was glad that Blanche would refuse my gesture. It somehow made sense that she wouldn't want my help with Grace.

Blanche stood and looked out the window for a moment.

"I'm keeping Grace out of school for a week or so. I'll make arrangements to change her bus route when I call the principal about her schoolwork."

I sat in stunned silence for a moment before I managed a shaky, "Good. Then that's settled."

Blanche cleared her empty cup off the table and started in on the dishes. I took my coffee to the front porch.

I had never questioned my benevolence before. I was raised on the Scriptures. I knew what Jesus said about doing "unto the least of these". Doing a kind thing was part of my nature and wasn't it a kind thing to allow Blanche's child to stay with her every day? So why, suddenly, did it seem as if the gift had come from Blanche?

Grace woke up thirty minutes later. She wandered onto the porch with her hair stuck straight out on one side and a crease on her cheek where it had rested on the table. She stared at me for a moment, then climbed into my lap as if she had sat there a hundred times before.

"Mama said to come keep you company."

I patted her leg and we sat quietly watching the squirrels in the pecan trees until Blanche came to get Grace to take a bath. While she was in the tub, I walked to the JC Penney store downtown and bought a new outfit, complete with shoes and socks, for Grace. I came home to find Grace wrapped in a huge towel, sitting on the bed in the guest room. Blanche was rolling up Grace's soiled clothing and putting it into a paper sack.

"What are you going to do with those?" I asked. I think part of me still hoped she'd call the police. I couldn't imagine not reporting such a horrible violation as Gracie had endured.

"I'm not sure," she replied.

"Don't wash them yet." I said, and prepared for the backlash I was sure would come.

"Hadn't planned on it," Blanche said.

Five

It was amazing how quickly things went back to normal, if you can ever call your life normal after such an event has taken place. Blanche told Grace that her ordeal had been nothing more than a bad dream. It's not how I'd have handled it, but that's probably not saying much under the circumstances.

As October settled in, Eddie stopped mowing my dormant St. Augustine grass and spent his time raking leaves, gathering pecans and mulching my flower beds with pine straw. A home as old as mine needed frequent upkeep and there were always odd jobs to do. Eddie seemed grateful for the extra money and completed each task with extraordinary care. He generally showed up early and left before Grace got off the bus in the afternoon.

Grace settled into her new routine and easily made herself at home, despite Blanche's frequent admonitions to mind her manners and stay out of my hair. Blanche needn't have worried and I told her so. Grace was precocious and curious, but not at all destructive and I enjoyed her company more than her mama would have imagined. She turned out to be a blessing, in more ways than one.

When Halloween rolled around, I got to sit and enjoy the Trick-or-Treaters going from house to house. Grace, filled with self-importance and utter glee in the witch's costume I made for her, stood at the edge of the stoop and counted out exactly two pieces of candy for each child.

The pigtails Blanche kept in Grace's hair prevented a good fit for the pointed black hat I got at Woolworth's. Each time she reached into the plastic pumpkin that held the candy, the hat tipped forward, rolling off her head and down the front steps. Blanche and I sat in our rockers on the porch and laughed until our sides ached watching that child. She wouldn't hear of taking the hat off until I suggested she pour the candy from the pumpkin into the hat and distribute it that way.

When the foot traffic slowed, Blanche gathered Grace up and headed for home. Grace put up a fuss until Blanche promised to stop at a few houses on the way so she could collect some candy of her own. I refilled the pumpkin bucket and sat awhile longer on the porch to wait for latecomers.

Blanche and Grace had only been gone a few minutes when Skipper Kornegay showed up with three of his friends in tow. They were too old for costumes, but apparently not too proud to stand in line for candy.

"Hey, Miz Beckworth."

"Hey, yourself."

I wasn't in the mood for hypocrisy.

"Nice evening, ain't it?"

"It was."

He gave a nervous laugh.

"Well, uh…Trick or Treat."

"Aren't you a little old for Trick-or-Treating?"

"Yeah, well, you're never too old for candy, Miz Beckworth."

He laughed again. I didn't.

"I think you're wrong there, Skipper. Comes a time when you have to put away childish things and face life like a man."

His friends, to this point standing in silence, began to laugh uneasily, too. I called them each by name.

"Donnie Allred. You old enough to be treated like a man?"

"Yes'm, I reckon I am."

"Then you don't need any candy, now do you?"

"No ma'am, I don't reckon I do."

"Allen Madison. You old enough to be treated like a man?"

"My daddy don't think so." He elbowed Skipper, who was the only one of the four who no longer laughed.

"James Robert Hardy, you old enough to be treated like a man?"

Allen answered for him. "Jimbo's still in diapers, Miz Beckworth. I think he should still get some candy."

Jimbo turned and walked away. "Come on, y'all. Let's get outta here."

Skipper didn't move, nor take his eyes from mine. The other three boys turned and laughed their way down the sidewalk, pushing and heckling each other, no doubt wondering what had gotten into this crazy old lady. Skipper stayed put.

"You got something to say to me, son?"

"I could ask the same of you." His voice held more contempt than fear. I stood my ground anyway.

"*Are* you asking, Mr. Kornegay?"

Silence.

"I didn't think so."

Knowing what he had done to Grace, I probably should have been afraid, but I wasn't. Skipper was defiant, but puzzled. It occurred to me that he had not made the connection between Grace and me. I wanted to confront him right there. Wanted to call his daddy and tell him to come pick up his deviant son and do something about him. But my loyalty was to Blanche and I bit my tongue.

I stared at him for several minutes until, finally, he fidgeted a bit and looked away. I pulled a handful of candy from the bucket and tossed them on the ground at Skipper's feet.

"Here's your candy, boy."

I turned my back on him and went into the house, flipping the porch light off as I did. Moments later I heard the clatter of wrapped candy hitting the front window like hail. I don't know when he left or which direction he went. I went to bed and picked up the candy the next day.

By the time we started making preparations for Thanksgiving, Blanche's entire family had gotten used to the changes in our relationship. It wasn't unusual now for Blanche's twins, ReNetta and Danita, to show up of an afternoon, just to do their homework on the front porch or watch T.V., which they didn't have at home. Patrice had made the cheerleading squad at the high school, so she was no longer home in the afternoon to watch them anyway.

One of the mixed blessings of living on Main Street is having a front row seat for all of the local parades. I never tired of seeing the homemade floats made from chicken wire stuffed with colorful paper napkins. And, though the very thought of having a child of my own in a beauty pageant sent me into fits of revulsion, I secretly enjoyed waving at the little girls perched on the backs of sporty convertibles. I could even forgive the mothers who dressed them in layers of tulle and satin, curled their hair into tiny ringlets and plastered their sweet faces with enough makeup for three grown women when I thought about how wonderful it must feel to be a princess for a day.

The closest I ever came was the day I was married. That went by so quickly that, when you factor in my nerves, I was left with not much more than a long list of do's and don'ts and thank you notes etched in my memory of the event.

This year's homecoming parade was particularly exciting for the girls. Patrice would be leading the Mayville High Cheerleading Squad. I helped take up her uniform at the beginning of the year. The skirt was a little short, but I have to admit Patrice was striking in it. Her long dark legs contrasted beautifully with the orange and white pleats of the skirt and she carried her willowy body with extraordinary grace. She was then and remains today, a simply beautiful girl.

Blanche's children had seen many a parade from the porch of my house, but never one with their own sister in such a prominent role. They had school banners to wave and spent hours practicing the chants they'd watched Patrice learn at the beginning of the season.

The parade started at 4:00 p.m. on Homecoming Friday. The game would start at 7:00 that night, but none of us would be going. I think Blanche always wanted to go see Patrice cheer, but I imagine the thought of negotiating those wooden bleachers was enough to give her pause. We were all excited for the opportunity to see her in action.

Blanche put on a pot roast for supper and settled us on the porch with sweet tea, Kool-aid and popcorn. The fall weather was perfect for a parade. I do not ever experience the metamorphosis of summer to fall without hearing the distant sound of marching bands and police sirens in my head.

I should have been prepared, should have thought ahead to what might happen but, as usual, I didn't and the day was nearly ruined before it even got off to a good start.

First in line in every hometown parade is always the police chief, followed by squad cars of various officers not on duty at the time.

Blanche had gone in to check the roast. Danita and ReNetta were standing on the sidewalk, with Gracie hopping about on the flat stoops at the base of the columns flanking the porch steps. She might not have even looked up if Ralph Kornegay hadn't chosen the moment he passed our house to flip on his blaring siren. Gracie squealed and covered her ears, then craned her neck to see the source of the commotion. There, waving from the front seat of his father's squad car, sat Skipper Kornegay, his white hair gleaming in the low pitch of the afternoon sun.

Gracie flattened herself against the porch column, hands reaching behind to grip its wide round girth, her face a mask of terror and her feet back pedaling as if she could push the column out of the way with her body.

I don't remember a time when I moved so swiftly. I was out of my chair within seconds, my glass of tea cast aside without thought. I reached Gracie just as the scream penetrated her paralyzed vocal chords and joined the sound of the wailing siren. Scooping her up under one arm, I flung open the screen door and entered the living room, kicking the heavy wooden door shut with one foot. Both doors slammed at once.

Blanche met me at the hallway and took Grace from me without a word. I don't remember if I ever even told her what happened. I think she just knew from the sound of the scream that it was another nightmare come back to haunt her little girl.

Blanche took Grace into the guest room and worked to quiet her down. A wave of nausea hit me with the force of a hurricane and I stumbled to the downstairs bathroom, my fingers shaking too violently to manage the light switch. I don't know how long I vomited or how many times, but by the time I felt able to walk again, Blanche's crooning had worked its magic and Grace was asleep under the chenille bedspread, bathed in that now familiar pink glow.

Six

We missed seeing Patrice's squad pass by the house and her disappointment was obvious when she popped in to eat dinner before the game.

"Mama!" Patrice complained. "Where were you?"

As Blanche struggled to respond, the twins mercifully provided a plausible, if not completely accurate, reason for our absence.

"Aw, that ol' sireen scared Gracie half to death," Danita put in first.

"Yeah, you shoulda seen it," ReNetta said, rolling her eyes. "Miz Ora had to carry her inside, hollerin' like a little baby."

Patrice's annoyance quickly turned to concern.

"Is she okay?" she asked Blanche.

"She fine," Blanche answered. "She been sleepin' ever since."

"I'm worried about her, Mama," Patrice said. "She hasn't been herself lately."

"Don't you worry none." Blanche tried to reassure her. "She go'n be all right. She jus' tired, that's all."

"She's been tired a lot," Patrice persisted.

"You best stop your fussin' and eat up now. Game starts in half an hour."

The rest of our meal passed in silence and Grace did not wake until Blanche put her into the taxi to go home.

It was a while before I got used to the constant commotion in the house each day after school, but I took to taking a nap after lunch, so I'd at least be rested up for the afternoon onslaught of laughing and squabbling. The twins often asked me for help with their homework. They seemed to be in awe of the fact that I had been to college. They were puzzled, however, as to why I had never actually taught school, as I had intended to do with my degree in Home Economics.

Up until that point, I had never questioned it myself. Sometimes it seemed like I was listening to the story of my own life and not telling it when I explained to the girls how different it was for women "way back then". Don't get me wrong. I've had a nice life and Walter was good to me for all practical purposes. It's just that their questions made me wonder how my life might have been different if I'd lived it for myself and not for the man I married.

I remember one of those conversations vividly. It had been decided that Blanche's entire family including Marcus, who would be home on leave from the Army, would have dinner at my house for Thanksgiving. It was the first year we would do such a thing. Every year before, I had given Blanche a turkey and a ham, an extra twenty-five dollars in her paycheck and four days off for the holiday. By the standards of the day that was rather generous for hired help and it made me feel good, benevolent soul that I was.

Walter and I always ate dinner out after serving at the Episcopal Church's benefit meal. Walter, an insurance agent and local philanthropist, used every opportunity he could to make contacts in the community. Charitable events were his thing and my job was to help coordinate the details and then show up in a nice dress. I was never a great beauty, but I cleaned up well.

The twins helped me polish the silver for Thanksgiving dinner. They wanted to know all about the silver and why we were spending so much time polishing it for use at only one meal. ReNetta was the more inquisitive of the two, although in all other ways the two were identical and I had yet to find a way to tell them apart.

"These sure are some pretty forks, Miz Beckworth."

"They belonged to my mother," I said. "She gave them to me when I married Mr. Beckworth in 1941."

"Dang! That's a long time ago."

"Mmm...thirty-five years," I agreed.

"How many times you reckon you used 'em since then?"

"Oh, I don't know. Not so many times lately, but fairly often when I was younger and Mr. Beckworth was trying to make a name for himself in Mayville."

"What's silverware got to do with that?" ReNetta asked.

"What, indeed!" I thought, but then I snorted a little and replied genially, "Back then, it was important to be a good hostess. Wives played a big role in their husbands' success in the business world."

"How come?"

I thought about this a minute. It was a perfectly reasonable question and it had a perfectly reasonable answer. I was sure of it.

"Well, it's important to meet the right people if you want to increase your business."

"Can I have some more polish, please?" Danita spoke up from the other end of the table. She had finished her stack of serving pieces. The quiet ones always finish first, I've learned.

"'*May* I have some more polish?' is how you ask that question, Danita."

I ignored the roll of eyes as I passed the jar of silver polish to ReNetta and nodded toward her twin sister. ReNetta held it out for Danita, but kept on with the conversation.

"So, you used the silverware to meet people?" ReNetta had a knack for making me feel ridiculous, although I'm certain that was not her intent. She was genuinely puzzled by the whole idea.

"Okay, Miss Nosy, enough with the questions. I'm going to tell you a story. You just listen and then, if you have any questions, I'll be happy to try to answer them."

"You gonna tell a story?" Danita perked up at her end.

"Mmm-hmm. That okay?"

"Is it one Grace can hear? She likes stories." Danita was the more maternal twin, always thinking of her little sister and trying to include her in things. ReNetta didn't intentionally leave anyone out. It was just that she was a bit single-minded by nature.

"Grace is more than welcome to listen, although it may be a little boring for her."

Danita was out of her seat before I finished speaking. She dashed from the room nearly causing Blanche to drop the armload of linens she was bringing into the dining room.

"Whoa!" was all Blanche could manage.

"'Scuse me, Mama," Danita threw over her shoulder. "I gotta get Grace. Miz Beckworth's gonna tell us a story."

Blanche raised an eyebrow at me. "They botherin' you, Miz Ora?"

"Not a bit," I replied honestly.

It was Blanche's turn to snort before she turned around and headed back for the kitchen.

When Grace and Danita were settled back down at the table, I began to tell my story.

"I met Walter Beckworth in 1938, when I was home from college for my father's funeral. Walter was new in the insurance business, but he had inherited my father's account and was helping my mother with the paperwork to collect on Daddy's life insurance policy. Daddy died unexpectedly and Mother had never dealt with paperwork of any kind before.

"Needless to say, she was a bit overwhelmed. Now, I was perfectly capable of helping her with it, but when I saw how kind and honest Walter was, I stepped back and let him handle everything for her. As a matter of fact, I remember pretending to be a little overwhelmed by it myself, just so Walter would show up more often. I think that's when I knew Walter had the potential to be my husband. I'd never met a man who could make me feign ignorance when my intellect was my greatest pride."

"You sure use a lot of big words, Miz Beckworth." It was Grace's turn to make me feel silly.

"Nothing wrong with using big words, Grace."

"Except if you don't understand 'em."

"Which ones didn't you understand?"

"All of 'em."

"Perhaps I'd better get to the point, then."

"Yeah, perhaps."

Grace wrinkled her nose and grinned. She may not have understood the words I was using, but she sure did know how to tease an old lady.

"Grace!" Danita was horrified.

"Shhhh!" ReNetta just wanted to hear the story.

"Okay, where was I?"

"You met Mr. Beckworth and decided to marry him." ReNetta was as concise as she was curious.

"It wasn't exactly that fast, ReNetta. He courted me for a year before he asked me to marry him."

"And when did you?" ReNetta asked. "Marry him, I mean."

"Not right away. I finished college first."

"Why'd you do that? Weren't you just going to get married and live happily ever after?"

"Well, I certainly hoped so, but I did have the good sense to know that things could happen. My father was not old when he died, remember. I think that had the most to do with my finishing my degree. I could always teach if being a wife and mother didn't work out."

I hesitated then. Motherhood hadn't worked out for me. My empty womb had made me doubt myself in ways I hadn't imagined were possible. That was another story, however, and certainly not one for young children.

"You a mother, Miz Beckworth?" Leave it to ReNetta to leave no stone unturned.

"No, ReNetta, I was never blessed with children."

"You didn't have no babies at all?" Grace looked at me with innocent surprise. My stomach pinched into a tiny knot.

"Not a one." I smiled feebly and sighed.

"I'm sorry," was Grace's reply.

"Me, too." I took a deep breath. "But, we were talking about silverware, not children, weren't we?"

Grace flopped her elbows onto the table and rested her face in both hands. It gave her a comical expression with her mouth pulled into a wide flat-lipped grin and her eyes twinkling behind three rolls of cheek pushed high on her face. I laughed out loud.

"But, if I'd had a child, I'd want her to be just like you, Gracie-love."

She wiggled happily in her seat and pushed her cheeks even higher.

"Okay, let's see," I searched my ever-fading memory. "Mr. Beckworth and I married in June of 1941. It was right after my graduation from Agnes Scott College in Atlanta. My mother had to plan most of the wedding without me, but that didn't bother me a bit. I never was big on pomp and circumstance, but I'd go along with just about anything Mother said was the right thing to do."

"What's pop and circus hands?" Grace demanded.

"Pomp and circumstance," I corrected. "It means fancy stuff."

"Oh," she sighed.

"Grace, hush!" ReNetta complained. "We're never gonna hear this story if you keep askin' so many questions."

I continued, "I picked out my china pattern and a wedding dress when I was home on spring break and got home from graduation just in time to have a bridal shower and help my attendants get fitted for their dresses. Mother picked out the flowers and everything else."

"Was it pretty?" Danita wanted to know this. Danita, the dreamer, I was coming to know.

"I thought so. But, mostly it was suitable. Suitable for a young lady from a good Southern family. The right china patterns, the right customs, the right number of bridesmaids and the right food at the rehearsal dinner. I was a suitable bride for a suitable man."

"Sounds kinda boring to me," ReNetta grunted.

"I honestly didn't think so," was my bemused reply.

"So, what's all this got to do with silverware?" ReNetta was not going to let up at all.

"Well, the silverware was just part of the whole thing. When you got married, you had things you just did, like the things I told you about. You got fine china and your mother's silverware pattern and you went from being someone's daughter to being someone's wife and then that had its own set of expectations, which you just fulfilled, same as everything else."

"Were you happy?" Danita wanted to know.

"Well, of course I was happy," I replied. "What's not to be happy about?"

"You never said why you only used the silverware sometimes, though."

"Too much work," I replied a little too sharply.

"So how come we're using it for Thanksgiving?" Grace quite logically asked. I sighed and shook my head.

"Some things are worth the effort," was all I could think to say.

Seven

Thanksgiving that year was the first time in a long, long time that I filled my house with so many happy, laughing people. Marcus arrived home on Wednesday, and on Thursday the whole troop of Lowerys arrived on my doorstep at 10:00 a.m.

Blanche and I had baked pies the day before and the turkey was stuffed and ready to be put in the oven. Marcus found several things to do around the house which I felt certain Blanche had mentioned to him in advance. Patrice set the table as if she had been doing it for years. Blanche had obviously been attentive to her training all along, if Patrice's confidence were any indication. The twins were charged with entertaining Grace, which they happily did. Close to noon, Blanche appeared in the doorway of my living room where I had retired to rest my feet.

"Reckon Eddie has anywhere to go today?"

I felt a sudden twinge of guilt. It had been over a month since my yard had been mowed for the last time that year. I had offered to find a few things around the house to keep Eddie busy, but he had allowed as how he might take a few months off to rest. I hadn't argued and assumed he was doing exactly as he said.

"I hadn't thought of it, Blanche, but I'm sure there's something going on at one of the churches. The Episcopals still have their event every year."

Blanche dried her hands on the towel she was holding. "That's clear across town."

"What are you getting at, Blanche? Do you want to invite him to dinner here?"

"Well, not exactly, but I was thinking maybe Marcus could take him a plate later on."

"He could, but wouldn't it be kinder to just ask him here to eat?"

"He may not be comfortable with that, Miz Ora."

"Why don't we give him the option?"

So, that's what we did. Marcus was dispatched to the general area of the old man's living quarters, if you could call it that. He reappeared a half hour later with the news that Eddie would indeed like to join us and would be along in an hour or so. I must say I was a little surprised at that, seeing as how the man had never ventured past the left corner stoop of my house.

An hour later he showed up looking somehow neater than I remembered. His face was clean shaven and his hair so closely cropped that you could see the distinct tiny curls of gray and white that littered his scalp like a field of dandelion. They looked equally fragile, too, as if one good puff of air might blow them all away. Gone was the cap in hand, gone the threadbare shirt. If I hadn't known better, I'd have thought he'd gotten a real job and a roof over his head somewhere. But Marcus had found him where he always stayed, so I knew that wasn't the answer.

"I'm so glad you could make it. Won't you come in?"

I assumed my hostess role by habit I suppose, despite the fact that I had relieved myself of all duties the moment Walter was laid in the ground. I had always assumed we would retire together, but Walter worked right up until the moment he succumbed to a massive heart attack in the men's room at the Rotary Club downtown. Bless his heart, he hadn't even managed to pull his pants up before he slumped to the floor in front of the toilet. It was an undignified ending for such a fastidious and dignified man and I hadn't quite gotten over that yet. I decided to retire immediately. I told myself it had nothing to do with having to face all the whispers at the Woman's Club and the Ladies' Auxiliary. I imagine I wasn't the only one who felt relieved by that decision.

Anyway, there I was with a homeless man as a guest in my home. My instincts took over and I did my best to make him comfortable. We chatted as we made our way to the living room.

"Thank you, Miz Beckworth. I 'preciate the invite, I sho do. I wasn't lookin' forward to walkin' 'cross town to the shelter for Thanksgiving dinner."

"You're most welcome, Eddie. I'm delighted to have you."

Was that what I was? Delighted? It didn't really seem to fit. Pleased to have him? Maybe. Certainly not displeased; I was glad he wouldn't go hungry today. Come to think of it, I was rather pleased. Pleased with myself for not hesitating in my offer. Pleased that Blanche had not successfully called my bluff, whether she intended that or not. Pleased that I had been tested and passed.

I did a quick mental comparison of this particular feeling of pleasure and the one I felt each year before, when I had helped plates down at the Episcopal Church's Annual Thanksgiving charity meal. It's easy to feel benevolent when you're wearing an apron and gloves over a Chanel suit and dishing out turkey and dressing to a long line of the "least of these."

This was different. I'm not sure I would have invited Eldred Mims to my home for Thanksgiving if I hadn't been backed into this corner and that's just the plain truth. But, there he was and there I was and, by God, I had an audience. I wasn't about to fall on my face.

"We're planning on eating at two, Eddie. I hope you're not starving..."

My voice trailed off helplessly. I generally keep my feet out of my mouth when I'm entertaining, but this one was wedged in tight. I didn't even try to take it out.

"I'll be right back. I need to check on Blanche's progress and see if she needs any help."

Eddie did not reply, but if I wasn't mistaken, I'd swear there was a twinkle in his eye that I had never seen before. And I'm dead positive I heard him chuckle when I left the room.

We sat down to Thanksgiving dinner promptly at 2 p.m. Marcus sat at one end of the long formal dining table and I at the other end. I had intended to do place cards, but didn't, and Grace had that under control anyway. Directly at my left sat Grace, who had established that seating arrangement immediately upon learning that it was her personal responsibility to keep me company. She sat "Mr. Pecan", as she called him, on the other side of herself and directly across from her mother. Patrice was to my right and the twins sat on either side of Marcus at the other end. Eight of us—just right for my old mahogany table, which had scarcely been used in the past forty years and possibly never used to seat an entire family at once.

Blanche set a steaming bowl of giblet gravy on the table and took her seat. Hands immediately reached out to each other around the table. I took a deep breath. I had never prayed aloud that I could remember. Walter had always done that for us. After his death, I mostly ate alone and so I bowed my head and thanked God silently before every meal. I suddenly couldn't remember the etiquette for this situation. All I could manage was, "Who would like to say Grace for us?"

Grace sputtered, "Why you want somebody to say my name?"

Blanche jumped in with, "Hush, child!"

Marcus looked flustered and deferred to Blanche, who closed her eyes, took a deep breath, opened her eyes, breathed out and said gently, "Eddie, would you please ask the blessing for us?"

Of all the silly notions... I couldn't believe Blanche would do such a thing to that poor old man. Why, she couldn't possibly know if he even believed in God, much less worshiped Him.

Eddie nodded, his voice cracking slightly as he began, "Father God, have mercy on us po' sinners gathered before you on this fine, fine day. Father, we are grateful for this food and for these friends and we ax' yo' blessin' on us all." His voice gathered strength with each word and I was reminded of the evangelists I heard on television. There was a pleasant rhythm to the way he spoke, and not just because of the sharp smacking noises that provided percussion to his words.

"Forgive us, Father, for our transgressions and keep us mindful of yo' sacrifice every single day. Lawd, make us truly thankful for all these things you have done, in Jesus' name, Amen."

"Amen!" was the chorus that preceded the next thirty minutes of feeding frenzy. Marcus carved the turkey as if he had been doing that task for years, and he probably had. Grace chattered happily to her new friend, the Pecan Man. If the events of two months prior had any lasting effect, you wouldn't know it by the way Grace responded to Eddie.

Blanche had convinced the child that her horror in September was all a bad dream. That was how she had handled it with her other children as well. Grace had had a bad dream and it frightened her terribly, so no one was to discuss it. End of story. I wasn't convinced it was a good way to deal with the situation, but it seemed to be working for now.

I was a little overwhelmed by the noise at the table at first, but I was soon laughing heartily at the antics of Grace and the twins and the stories that Marcus shared of life at boot camp.

I finally got around to asking Eddie where he'd been for the past few weeks. Seems his daughter had sent him a bus ticket to come to Alabama for a visit. I asked why he didn't just stay down there, but he offered little in the way of explanation.

"Some things just ain't meant to be, Miz Beckworth. We's both better off not bein' too close."

"That must be hard for you."

"Not really," he replied with a shrug. "We ain't never had too much in common. This here some good cawnbread dressin' Miz Blanche. You make this?"

Moves like that didn't bode well for my prying. I focused on eating my cranberry gelatin.

After dinner Blanche and Patrice cleared the table, Grace and the twins turned on the television set in the living room and the two men and I retired to the porch. Eddie seemed to be anxious to get home, but Blanche was packing him up some leftovers to take with him. Not too much, for it wouldn't keep without refrigeration, even with the nights turning cooler now.

The three of us rocked in silence for quite a while. I think back to those moments now and I realize just how quickly whole lives can be altered. Sometimes, it's just a few words here or there that put things in motion and everything you believe about yourself changes. Things you couldn't have dreamed you'd do are done in the blink of an eye.

If Blanche had packed faster, if Marcus had headed upstairs to finish fixing that leaky faucet, if I had never invited Eldred Mims to Thanksgiving dinner, Skipper Kornegay might still be alive today.

"How's dat l'il girl doin'?"

The question from Eldred came out of the blue. I half-choked on my tea and sputtered, "Who, Gracie?"

"I felt awful bad 'bout what happened to her. I didn't hardly know what to do but bring 'er on home that day I found 'er."

Marcus was leaning forward in his chair with an expression on his face that even I couldn't read. It was shock, I suppose.

"You found her?" I blurted out. I suppose I should have been able to cover better than I did, but I had never asked Blanche how the child got home that day. I just assumed she had come of her own accord and Blanche had not wanted to speak of any of the details.

"Yeah, I's the one what found her, cryin' fo' her mama like she was. I like to never got to sleep that night f' worryin' 'bout that chile."

"Found her where?" Marcus found his voice. "What's he talking about, Miz Beckworth?"

Now it was Eddie's turn to look shocked. I was equally stunned and I just sat with my mouth half-opened for a minute. I hadn't been prepared to tell an outright lie and, at that moment, all my upbringing screamed, "Don't!" Unfortunately, I couldn't tell if that meant don't *lie* or don't *tell*. So, with my heart beating that one single word, I said, "Oh, Gracie just had an accident, that's all."

"What kind of accident?" Marcus demanded to know.

"I think I done talked outta turn," Eddie managed. "I thought the family knowed all about it."

"Blanche didn't want to worry anyone, is all." My voice quaked under the strain of lying.

"What happened to Gracie, Miz Beckworth? I thought she just had a bad dream about something."

"Marcus, you're gonna have to talk to your Mama about this."

Eddie stood. "I got to go. I'm sorry, Miz Beckworth. I didn't mean no harm."

"Wait, Eddie. Blanche is packing your food."

"No, I got to go."

He was off the porch and halfway down the sidewalk when Blanche appeared at the door with a Winn Dixie bag packed with leftovers for Eddie to take with him.

"Where's he…"

"What happened to Grace, Mama?" Marcus clenched and unclenched his fists with nervous energy.

"Oh, Lord, help me," was all Blanche could manage before she sunk into the nearest chair and dropped the sack of food to the floor.

It happened so fast, I still wasn't sure how much damage had been done. I wracked my brain to remember every word that had been said in case Blanche could stick with her dream story without Marcus being certain she was lying. Blanche looked up at me with that very question on her face. *How am I going to do this?*

Not being privy to the whole discussion, Blanche had no clue how to proceed. I tried to fill in for her, but as is probably already apparent, I'm not altogether quick on my feet.

"Eddie was just asking after Gracie, Blanche. He wanted to know how she was doing after she had that accident and he brought her on home."

"Oh," Blanche nodded, "the accident." She wasn't particularly convincing if you ask me.

"Gracie just fell over some rocks on her way over to Miz Ora's house and Eddie was kind enough to bring 'er on home to us, tha's all."

"What rocks?" Marcus wasn't buying a word of it.

"I don't know what rocks, Marcus. Just some rocks out in the woods," Blanche broke out in beads of sweat across her forehead.

"What was she doing in the woods?"

"She was takin' a shortcut, I suppose."

"Gracie knows better'n to take any shortcuts, Mama. Besides, I played in every stick of any woods we got close by and there ain't a rock in 'em that's big enough to trip over. Now, somebody better tell me what happened to Grace and they better tell me now."

I raised my hands in a gesture that clearly said *don't look at me!*

Blanche raised herself out of the chair, wiped a forearm across her face.

"Don't be makin' such a fuss outta nothin', Marcus. Gracie fell. That's all they is to it."

Marcus stood, too, rising a full foot over the compact bulk of his mother. I watched the fear and anger wash over him like a baptism. I can't imagine how much it hurt that boy to stand there and hear his mama tell him what he knew was a lie.

He hesitated for a moment, then turned and headed off in the same direction as Eldred Mims. We hoped he might be headed home, but he wasn't and we should have known that. We should have known.

Eight

Blanche was solemn and quiet as she put away the last of the dishes and prepared to walk the two miles home. By the time they got there, it would be six-thirty and turning cool with the setting sun.

"Want me to call you a cab?"

"Naw, we all right, Miz Ora. Night air do us good."

I suddenly felt silly for never having gotten a driver's license. My father disapproved of young women driving and, once I married Walter, I had no need to learn how. His Ford LTD was still sitting in the garage. It sat in the parking lot of the Rotary Club for nearly a week after his death before a fellow Rotarian thought to bring it home.

"Really, Blanche, I don't mind paying for a cab tonight. There's a breeze kicking up and, well, let me call a cab for you. I'll be right back."

Blanche might have argued, but Grace fussed as Patrice zipped her jacket. She wasn't the only tired child. The twins yawned and fidgeted as they shifted leftovers from arm to arm. Blanche said nothing, so I called City Cab and gave them the address. The taxi arrived in minutes and the girls crowded into the back seat with Blanche taking the front. I gave Blanche a five to pay the driver and shut the door. I leaned into the open window and asked quietly, "What are you going to do about Marcus?"

"He'll be all right," she said softly. "He's prolly out somewhere blowin' off steam. He'll be fine. What he don't know can't hurt him. That's just all there is to it."

"Thanks for today, Blanche. That was the best Thanksgiving I've had in years."

"It was the onliest Thanksgivin' you had in years, Miz Ora."

"The only one with family, anyway."

I patted Blanche on the arm and stepped back from the curb and the taxi pulled away. The side mirror reflected Blanche's grin in the fading light and one dark arm reached out the window and gave a little wave as they turned the corner toward home.

I sat on the porch until the street lights flickered on, then went into the house and poured a glass of iced tea. I watched the evening news, and then I read for an hour or so until I felt sleepy. I had just turned off the porch light and locked up when I heard a commotion near the back door. It sounded like something had been thrown onto the stoop and then crashed into the bushes. I froze for a moment. The bushes rattled again and finally there was a low, insistent knocking on the door.

I looked at the clock. It was nearly nine-thirty. Long past the time when anyone should come calling, especially at the back door. My mind raced with unspoken questions. I couldn't remember where Walter kept that old pump-action Winchester he used to run the squirrels out of the pecan trees. Lot of good it would do me. I hadn't a clue how to fire it.

The knock sounded again, a little louder this time.

"Miz Beckworth? Miz Beckworth! It's me—Marcus!"

I could barely make out what he was saying, since he spoke in nothing more than a loud whisper. I peered out between the blinds covering the back door. Sure enough, I could tell it was Marcus from the sound of his voice and the shape of his head. I wrenched the door open and he stumbled inside. Looking at his face in the fluorescent light, I might not have recognized him at all. One eye was swollen shut and thick black dirt covered his hair and one cheek. I grabbed a kitchen towel from the counter, but I couldn't figure out what to do with it.

"What in heaven's name? Are you all right?"

"I'm in trouble, Miz Ora. Bad trouble."

"I'm callin' your mama."

"Oh, Lord, Miz Ora, please don't do that. It'll kill her. It'll kill her, what I done."

I saw then the ever-widening red stain on my linoleum floor. It was blood that held the dirt to his head, despite the steady flow. I tossed the towel onto the floor, as if mopping up the mess would stop the bleeding.

"What happened to you? Why are you bleeding?"

The more I stood gaping at him, the more I realized how serious this was. Marcus's right hand bled profusely. His shirt was saturated with blood and dirt. I flung a drawer open and pulled out several more towels. Marcus reached for one and I wrapped his hand with the largest, remembering finally the first aid I learned at the Ladies' Auxiliary. He winced and clutched the towel against his chest.

"This doesn't look good, Marcus. Don't you think I should call a doctor?"

"I don't know. I don't think so."

"Well, I need to call somebody! Do the police know about this?"

"No! Lord, no! And they cain't know. Oh, Miz Ora, what have I done? What have I done?" He looked at me then, as if he really expected me to answer him, but I had far too many questions of my own.

I pulled him to the sink and rinsed the dirt off his hands first, so I could see where to apply pressure. There was one deep cut below his thumb and several smaller wounds on his palm. I wrapped his hand tightly and told him to keep it that way. I was torn between the need to tend to his wounds and the desire to yank a knot in him and make him tell me what happened.

I forced his head over the sink and rinsed the dirt off with the spray nozzle. The matted mess had actually been helping to stem the flow and rinsing made the wounds bleed anew. I pressed a towel to the worst cut and pushed him toward the kitchen table. He stood, leaning on the table as I applied pressure to the wounds on his head.

"Are you hurt anywhere else?"

"No ... I don't know. I don't think so."

"You have to help me, son. How did you get hurt?"

"I went to find Eddie. I wanted to know what happened to Grace."

"Good Lord, Marcus, did he do this to you?" I couldn't imagine it, but anything seemed possible at the moment.

"No, Ma'am. He didn't even wanna talk to me, but I kept after him. Finally he told me somebody'd attacked her in the woods."

"Oh, Lord."

"I couldn't get it straight in my head, though. I thought he had just let it happen or something and I got really mad. God, I was so mad, I didn't know what to do." Marcus paced as he spoke. "I think I scared him pretty bad, 'cause he got real calm and told me to sit down, so I did." Then, as if obeying the command a second time, Marcus sat down at the table and finished his story.

"He told me he'd heard a commotion near where he stays and then he saw a couple of boys headed out of the woods. They were laughin' at another boy who was pulling up his pants and runnin' to catch up with 'em. He figured they just stopped to make water, like boys'll do, so he just turned around to go back. Then he said..." He paused then, his voice shaking with emotion.

"He said he thought he heard a ... a puppy cryin'—"

"Oh, dear Lord." I felt sick to my stomach.

"But it wasn't no puppy." Marcus tried to go on, but his entire body shook with the effort and no words came out.

I thought my heart would break right there. Blanche and I had not spoken of this. I hadn't wanted to ask. I didn't want to know.

Marcus took several ragged breaths and continued.

"He found Gracie, cryin' and tuggin' on her clothes. He said he didn't touch her, just walked her here to Mama, and Gracie told her what happened."

I remember thinking I'd never felt so tired in my life. My jaws ached and my ears burned from trying to hold back tears. We sat in silence for a few minutes, long enough to breathe again.

"Did Eddie tell you who raped Gracie?"

"He didn't want to," Marcus shook his head, "I swear, Miz Ora, I only meant to take the boy's name to the police, but once I learned who he was, I knew why Mama lied."

"I told her not to..."

"She couldn't do it no different, Miz Ora. That's the God's truth."

The boy was still bleeding on my table. I didn't have time to debate the particulars.

"You still haven't told me who hurt you. Did you have a fight with Skipper Kornegay? Is that why you don't want to call the police? Because I swear to you, Marcus. I'll make sure Ralph Kornegay treats you fairly. I tried to tell your mama the same thing..."

"No'm, that's not what I'm worried about, Miz Ora. I wish that was all it was, but it's not."

"Then, what is it, son?"

Marcus took a long, ragged breath and dropped his head onto the table with a wail of anguish I'd never in all my life heard. I could barely understand him through his sobs.

"I killed him, Miz Ora. Jesus help me, I killed him."

I don't know how long I sat there, stunned into silence, before I heard myself whisper, "You killed Skipper Kornegay?"

Marcus nodded, wiping his face on his arm as he did. Then, with his head still resting on the crook of his arm, he looked up at me. His jaw quivered and he drew in a few short, hiccoughing breaths and then grew calm.

"He's dead, Miz Ora."

I stood then, and walked into the kitchen on weak and shaky legs. I pulled two cups from the cabinet and poured water into the teakettle. I was buying time, I think ... time to consider what had to be done and in what order.

Skipper must have put up some kind of a fight to have caused the damage to Marcus's head and face, but I knew without having seen them together that Marcus was the stronger of the two.

I had to do something. But, I had to *think*. I finished brewing the two cups of tea and sat them both on the table. Marcus had not moved.

"Here's you some tea."

"I cain't drink nothin' right now."

"Yes, you can and you're going to," I commanded. "I need for you to compose yourself and tell me everything that happened."

"You gonna call the po-lice, Miz Ora?"

"I'm not calling anyone until I hear the whole story, but first I have to know something."

"Yes, Ma'am?"

"Are you positive he's dead? And I mean really positive, Marcus. I can't sit here and do nothing if he's out there somewhere needing help."

"He's dead, Miz Ora. Graveyard dead. I know 'cause I tried to wake him up when I got hol'ta myself, but he wasn't breathin' at all. I sat there for a long time prayin' he'd wake up or breathe or something, but finally I knew it was done. I heard a noise off in the woods and I ran. I didn't know where to go. I knew I couldn't run down Main Street lookin' like I did. So, I stayed in the woods as long as I could and came up in your back yard."

Then he told the rest of his story. I never had a doubt that Marcus told me the truth. He never hesitated and he never blamed anyone but himself for doing what he did.

When Marcus left Eldred Mims, he was beside himself with grief and fear. He wanted justice for Grace and punishment for Skipper, but he was scared of what would happen to his entire family if he went to the authorities. There seemed to be no way to do the right thing. He needed time to think, so he walked through the woods and out around the Minute Maid plant at the other end of Main Street.

He was coming back through town when he saw Skipper and his friends coming out of the door of the local pool hall.

"I saw them boys and I got mad all over again. But there was four of them and only one of me. So, I ducked into the alley behind the drug store. My heart was beatin' so fast, I thought it was gonna jump out my chest."

He said he waited until the boys' laughter grew faint and then he waited ten minutes more.

"There was so much hate inside me, I was burnin' up with it. But still," he added softly, "I jus' couldn't put Grace through somethin' worse than what she already suffered. I figured I'd best steer clear for now."

"Your mama said the same thing."

"I wish she hadn't lied to me. That hurt me the worst. I ain't never known her to lie straight out."

"She never meant to hurt you, Marcus."

"I know that. And I'd made my peace with it in those ten minutes. Army say it done made a man outta me, so I decided to go home a man. I was go'n tell Mama I knew she did what she had to do. But, the more I thought about my mama, the more I just wanted her to wrap her arms 'round me and tell me everything was go'n be all right, like she did when my daddy died."

I thought about my own mother then, and how much I would have loved to have her hold me that way.

Marcus stepped out of the alley just as Skipper Kornegay crossed the street and stepped onto the curb, less than ten feet from where Marcus now stood. He said they both jumped like they'd grabbed a cow fence.

"Shit!" Skipper bellowed. "Boy, you scared the piss outta me. What the hell are you doin' sneakin' outta there like that?"

"I ain't sneakin' nowhere."

"Looked like you was sneakin' to me. You got some business back there my daddy oughta know 'bout?"

"They's a lotta things your daddy *oughta* know 'bout, but I don't reckon you'd really want him to know everything 'bout everything."

"What the hell is wrong with you, boy?"

Marcus said he got really calm for a minute. He stood looking at Skipper Kornegay dead in the eye. Not blinking. Not wavering. Just staring. I remember thinking that was downright courageous of him, starin' a white man down. But, then I remembered that we'd come a long way since those days and that shouldn't really be anything notable.

Finally Marcus found his voice again. "Ain't nothin' wrong with *me*. Not a damn thing!"

"Boy, you what my daddy calls a' uppity nigger, ain'tcha?"

If I hadn't known before, I knew when I heard that. Blanche was right about Ralph Kornegay and I was a fool. I'd been in polite society so long that I took social graces for social conscience. We may not hear that word much in public anymore, but it doesn't mean it isn't said in private.

Marcus said he'd held his tongue all he could.

"If uppity means I don't take any shit off a child molester, then yeah, Skipper, I'm the uppity-est nigger you ever go'n meet."

"What the...?"

Marcus said Skipper had looked confused for a split second, until he made the connection with Grace. He laughed then.

I saw the anger rise up in Marcus when he recalled that part of the confrontation and I knew what he must have felt when he stood face to face with that monster.

"I wanted to smash his face into the sidewalk, Miz Ora," Marcus said through clenched teeth. "I knew right then I had to get away or I would do it. So help me, God, I would stomp him into the ground. I turned around and I ran—like a coward."

Marcus's face contorted with rage and shame. Listening to him then and knowing all I know to this day, I am absolutely certain that running was the most courageous thing he could have done at that moment, but you couldn't have told him that. He saw no honor at all in the act, only necessity. He wiped his face on his sleeve and went on with his story.

"I ran as fast as I could, Miz Ora, but it felt like my legs was made of cement. I could hear Skipper runnin' behind me, laughin' the whole way. I made it as far as the woods and ran far enough in that I thought I had lost him. I stopped to catch my breath and I listened for him to follow, but I didn't hear nothin' so I thought he'd gone on home."

"But, he didn't, did he?"

"No ma'am, he didn't," Marcus sighed. "I had barely calmed my breathin' down and all of a sudden he was just there, right in front of me. He was holdin' out his right hand and he threw his left one up in the air like he was sword fightin' or somethin'. I heard the click before I saw the blade. I hate knives, Miz Ora. Jesus help me, I hate 'em."

Marcus seemed resigned then. "I figured I was a dead man. I almost didn't even try to fight him off. If he'da come cut me up slow, I'da pro'bly let him. But he just jumped on me swingin' and so I fought him."

"Well, that's self-defense, Marcus! You fought him in self-defense. No court will convict you for that!"

"But, that's not all." Marcus dropped his chin to his chest and shook his head from side to side. "I don't remember what all happened, I swear I don't. I just remember doin' everything I could to keep him from hittin' me with that blade. I reckon he got me a few times anyway. I don't even remember tryin' to get the knife outta his hand; but all of a sudden, it was in mine. We wrestled around 'til my forearm was across't his neck and I was pressin' on his throat as hard as I could. He stopped fightin' for the knife and started grabbin' at my arm and that's when... Oh, Jesus..." Marcus wailed. He grabbed the back of his head in both hands and rocked back and forth.

"That's when *what*, son?"

Marcus stopped rocking and took a deep, wrenching breath. He looked me straight in the eye and delivered his confession.

"I stabbed him, Miz Ora. Over and over and over, I stabbed him. I don't even know how many times it was, but it wadn't no self-defense made me stab that boy like I did. It wadn't nothin' but pure hate and that's the truth."

He didn't shed another tear after that. He just laid his head on his arms and stared up at the table. I got up from my chair and put my arms around him, pulling him as tight to me as I could get. I wasn't his mama and my bony arms will never be called anything near soft, but I did what I could do to give him comfort.

Nine

I woke Marcus the next morning when the coffee finished brewing. He was nearly speechless in his sorrow, but I had no more time for comforting words. After he forced down two cups of coffee and was awake enough to listen carefully, I told him the plan I concocted through my largely sleepless night.

"We have to get you out of town before anyone sees you. Walter's car has enough fuel in it to get you at least three counties up the road, so you can stop at a gas station without being recognized."

"I can't take Mr. Walter's car, Miz Ora," Marcus protested.

"Why? You can drive, can't you?"

"Yes'm, I can drive. It's just that..." He looked incredibly uncomfortable, but I didn't have time to argue.

"Spit it out, son."

"Well, it just ain't really like you to let me take your car."

I stared at him hard for a minute, my fists pressing into the thin skin over my hip bones. He made a good point, no matter how much I wanted to deny it.

"You can make payments."

"But, where am I gonna go?"

"Just hush and listen. Then you can ask questions if you have them."

He nodded.

"I have enough cash for you to get a hotel room in Atlanta for the night. When you get up tomorrow morning, go straight back to Fort Bragg. When anyone asks, you can tell them you got into a fight in a bar."

"I don't know..."

I lost my patience.

"Do you have a better idea?"

"No ma'am, not really."

"You have options, Marcus. You can stay here and go to jail if you want to, but you asked for my help and I'm trying to give it to you. Do you want it or not?"

He fell silent and I finished giving him instructions. If questions ever arose, our stories would be the same: Marcus spent Thanksgiving night at my house, crying on my shoulder from 6:30 until midnight, and slept on my couch. Other than being upset with his mother, nothing seemed out of the ordinary, no visible wounds, no marks on his clothing. He never saw Skipper Kornegay and was nowhere near the woods where the boy was killed.

I persuaded Marcus to write his mother a note saying he'd talked to Eddie and was too upset to face her right now, but that he'd call her when he got back to Fort Bragg.

There were only two other people who might tell the story that connected Marcus and Skipper Kornegay, but I doubted Skipper's friends would implicate themselves in the rape of a child.

If Blanche had questions, I'd come up with answers. She'd been through a lot in the past few months and the last thing she needed was to watch her son go to prison for taking a child molester off the streets. I have consoled myself with that truth often over the years.

Marcus took a few more of Walter's clothes and accepted the turkey and dressing I packed for him. When he was ready, I followed him to the garage to get the car. As he turned the ignition, he rolled down the window and looked up at me with the one eye that wasn't swollen shut.

"I'm scared, Miz Ora."

"Me, too," I said.

He nodded then and put the car into reverse.

"Go over that story a thousand times while you're driving, son, and don't ever, *ever* change a word of it. No matter what anyone says."

He nodded again and backed down the driveway. I stood at the garage door and watched the LTD glide slowly down Main Street until it was out of sight. Then I turned and looked at the empty spot where Walter's car once sat. I have never felt more alone.

Looking back, I might have made better choices if I'd taken more time to consider. I spent my entire life doing only what I believed to be right and true. Yet, there I was, faced with the most crucial decision I would ever make and nothing remotely resembling the truth felt right. But, I had too much to do to stand there feeling sorry for myself. I closed the garage door and went back into the house.

I knew Blanche would be out of her mind with worry when Marcus didn't come home the night before, but I couldn't risk talking to her so soon after he left. I took the phone off the hook and got busy cleaning up every trace of evidence that Marcus was wounded when he showed up at my back door the night before.

Evidence. I remember using that word in my mind as I opened a new package of rubber gloves and got the bleach from the utility room. I was destroying evidence the police might use to solve a crime. I was taking justice into my own hands and, though I've wrestled with doubt since, I was downright fine with it then.

I finished mopping the kitchen floor, took the bucket of water and bleach and doused the back steps clean.

The clothes were a problem. They were torn and bloody and no amount of bleach or washing would render them clean. They would have to be burned. The nights were cool enough, but I hadn't taken to using the fireplace yet this year. I washed the bloody laundry with two cups of bleach to cover the smell and packed them away in a plastic bag, planning to burn them the first chance I got.

When I finished what I'd set out to do, I put on a fresh pot of coffee and headed upstairs to take a shower. I was drying off when I heard the front door open. I had barely gotten my robe on when I heard Blanche coming up the stairs, screaming for me at the top of her lungs.

"Miz Ora!" She waited only a couple of seconds and hollered again, "Miz Ora!"

"I'm coming, Blanche. Good Lord, what is the matter?" I was surprised at how quickly I slipped into my new role.

"Oh, Law', Miz Ora!" Blanche huffed and wheezed. "I thought you was dead!"

"Well, for heaven's sake, Blanche, of course I'm not dead! What in the world would make you say such a thing?"

Blanche mopped her face with a handkerchief.

"I been tryin' to get ahol'ta you all mornin', Miz Ora. What's the matter with your telephone?"

"Nothin's wrong with my phone, Blanche. It's off the hook. I've been trying to catch up on the sleep I lost sitting up with your boy half the night."

"Marcus? Marcus is here? Oh, thank you *Jesus!* I been outta my mind with worry."

"He *was* here, but he's gone now."

"Gone! But, he didn't come home. Where's he gone?"

"Long story. Blanche and I need some coffee to be able to tell it."

She followed me downstairs and into the kitchen.

"Smells like bleach in here."

Blanche doesn't miss a trick. In all the years she's been my housekeeper, she's never known me to mop. It's not one of my favorite chores.

"That's what I get for giving you the day off. I spilled a whole cup of coffee—*with* cream and sugar already in it. I figured I might as well mop the whole floor so it wouldn't be sticky all weekend."

The lie came amazingly easy.

"This is my second pot of coffee today. That boy of yours can sure talk once he has a mind to."

"I don't understand, Miz Ora. Why was Marcus here last night? Why didn't he come home? He's in trouble, idn't he?"

"You should have told him the truth about Grace. He went to find Eldred Mims when he left here, Blanche."

"Oh, Lord, no," she breathed.

"He didn't know everything when he came back, but he knew enough to be beside himself with grief. He came back to find you, but you and the girls had just left."

"Well, why didn't he just come on home then?"

"Marcus was very upset, Blanche. I wanted to calm him down first, and by the time we got through discussing the whole thing, I thought you were both better off if he stayed here to think things over."

"Well, you'd think somebody woulda called me and tol' me all this. I was worried sick about that boy. He ain't never done nothin' like this, not comin' home all night."

"He didn't want me to call, so I didn't."

Blanche was breathless and she sat heavily on the kitchen chair, still clutching and occasionally patting her broad chest.

"Where is he now?"

"He left you a note. He knew you'd be upset, but he needed time to think."

I handed her the note and watched her read it. When she finished, she laid the scrap of paper on the table, covered it with both hands, and sat staring out the window as she was inclined to do when she was thinking.

"Ain't right, Miz Ora. I know my boy and somethin' ain't right."

"Well, of course something isn't right, Blanche. The boy just found out his baby sister was raped and his mama lied to him about it. How would *you* feel?" I hated snapping at her like that, but her intuition frightened me.

"This thing jus' gets worse and worse, don't it? My mama always said lyin' was bad and she was right. I tried to teach that to all my babies, too. Once you tell a lie, you have to keep tellin' and tellin' and tellin' to make it stand."

I couldn't respond to that. I just looked down at my hands. We sat in awkward silence, each lost in unspoken thought and apprehension. She never had time to voice the questions I was prepared to answer with lies of my own. A knock at the front door saw to that.

I crossed the living room and opened the door, expecting to turn away an ill-timed sales pitch. The sight of two police officers made my heart gallop in my chest. In all my planning, I'd not expected this so soon.

"Mrs. Beckworth?" I recognized the speaker immediately. Barry Tinsley and his family attended our church.

"Barry?" I said, my voice already shaking. "What can I do for you?"

"I need to speak with Mrs. Lowery, Ma'am. Is she here today?"

I stepped aside and motioned toward Blanche, who was already on her feet.

"Mrs. Lowery," he said as he stepped inside the door and removed his hat. "Your son is Marcus Lowery, Ma'am?"

Blanche nodded, her eyes darting from Barry to me and back.

"I'm sorry, Mrs. Lowery. Marcus was killed in a car accident this morning on I-75."

Blanche hit the floor before he finished his sentence. She didn't utter a sound, just fainted dead away.

Ten

We buried Marcus beside his father, in the Mt. Zion A.M.E. Church cemetery. It was the first time I ever stepped foot in Blanche's church and I stuck out like a sore thumb. The service was not like any I ever attended, but I have no intention of describing it here. Of all the details I must give to satisfy my conscience before I die, there are some that will be left to the memories of those who were there. I owe Blanche this.

We may not ever know the exact details of Marcus's death. What we do know is this: on Friday morning, the day after Thanksgiving, Marcus was headed north on Interstate 75 when a trucker locked up the brakes on his tractor trailer rig to avoid a disabled vehicle in his lane. There were no skid marks on the highway to indicate that Marcus reacted at all. The hood of the car went beneath the trailer and the windshield took the full impact. Marcus was pronounced dead at the scene.

Blanche blamed herself, of course, but I knew I was the one who sent the boy to his death. I've lived with it every day since then. Blanche was right. Once a lie is told, you have to keep on telling it. You not only have to repeat it time and time again, you have to embellish it, layer upon layer until you don't even remember the truth. Every day I didn't tell Blanche what I knew was another day I lied to her. Guilt cloaked me like a wool blanket in summer and no amount of sweet tea or gentle ceiling fans ever soothed me again.

I begged Blanche to take some time off after the funeral, but she refused saying she could not bear to sit around her house and look at things that reminded her of Marcus. I could not tell her how well I understood. It was all I could do not to insist that she retire so I would not have the daily reminder of what I had done. But, even I recognized the cowardice in that and forced myself to go on.

Two days after Blanche buried her only son, Eldred Mims was arrested for the murder of Skipper Kornegay. Dovey Kincaid hightailed it over to tell me herself before I'd had a chance to read it in the morning paper.

"Miz Beckworth? Miz Beckworth!" She shouted as she banged her fist against the screen door.

I barely got the inside door unlocked and opened before she charged into my home without waiting for an invitation.

"Have you seen this?" she demanded, waving the Mayville Free Press under my nose.

"Why, Dovey Kincaid! I've been looking all over for that paper. Where'd you find it?"

"It was right there on your front step..." she began and stopped as my sarcasm dawned on her. "That's real funny, Ora Lee. You won't be laughing when you see what's on the front page. I tried to warn you about that awful old man, but did you listen to me? No, you did not!"

"What are you talking about, Dovey?"

"I told you he was dangerous, didn't I? He's the one killed Ralph Kornegay's son. It says so right here. They arrested him last night."

I snatched the paper from her and flipped it open. *Homeless Man Arrested for Murder of Police Chief's Son* read the bold headline.

"Oh, dear Lord." My hands shook so hard the paper crackled aloud.

"I'll say 'Dear Lord!'" Dovey huffed. "We could have all been killed. But you wouldn't hear a word of it. Harmless old man, you called him."

"Dovey, it's time for you to leave."

"Well, harmless, my foot! He's a cold-blooded killer, that's what he is! And you had him skulkin' around here big as you please. 'Won't hurt a fly,' you said."

"Get out of my house, Dovey," I warned again.

"He cut that boy to shreds is what he did! Pure shreds!" she said, wagging her finger in my face for emphasis. "Well, I wanna know what you have to say for yourself now, Miss Know-it-All."

To this day, I don't know what came over me. Maybe it was the schoolgirl tone of her name-calling that just pushed me over the edge. I rolled up that newspaper and popped Dovey Kincaid right in the head.

"Oh!" she screamed, throwing her hands up to cover her face.

"I *said* get out of my *house* and I *mean* get out of my *house!*" I punctuated my words with swats aimed at her perfectly coiffed hair.

"Oh! Oh! Oh!" she wailed as she bobbed and weaved to escape my blows. She fled through the front door with me on her heels. I stopped at the edge of the porch and watched her run blindly across the street, cupping her head in her arms and shrieking the whole way.

I stood there for a few moments puffing tiny clouds of fog into the cold December air as I tried to catch my breath. I turned to go back in and Blanche materialized at the screen door.

"Could you call me a cab?"

"Already did. Be here in ten minutes."

"You hear all that?"

"Ain't deaf yet, I reckon."

"Good Lord, what have I done?"

"Look like you done run that one off for good, I'd say."

I couldn't bring myself to tell her I wasn't talking about Dovey Kincaid.

I went straight to the police station and demanded to see Eddie. It was all I could do not to turn myself in immediately when I saw what they did to that pitiful old man. According to Ralph Kornegay, Eddie resisted arrest. That was the official account of the facial lacerations and bruises and the broken bones in his right arm. By the time I got to him, his bones were set and his wounds bound, but his attorney had not made it by to talk to him yet. That didn't surprise me a bit.

Eddie lay quietly on the lower bunk of the jail cell, his swollen face turned toward the wall. The sound of the key turning in the lock echoed loudly down the row of cells, but it did nothing to move him.

"Eddie?" I spoke softly first and when he didn't answer, a little louder. "Eddie? I've brought you some food."

He mumbled something then, but did not look up. The guard behind me spoke for him.

"He can't eat anything, Miz Beckworth. Can't hardly open his mouth."

"He has to eat, Mr. ... what was your name?" I asked and answered my own question by reading his nametag. "Mr. Smallwood. Oh! You Binky Smallwood's boy?"

"Yes, Ma'am."

That's the thing about southern boys; they can be mean as snakes and twice as deadly, but they're raised polite. This one didn't have a mean bone in his body, if memory served me correctly, but his father was a piece of work.

Binky Smallwood was a pompous little barrel of a man with six sons and an exhausted, but forgiving wife. He attended The Mayville Baptist Church every Sunday, but it was his Monday through Saturday habits that caused his unsuccessful bid for deaconship there. This was the youngest of the Smallwood crew, as Binky was fond of calling them. Binky was captain of his ship and he made sure everyone knew it.

Our pastor was a forward-thinking man who believed in Southern Baptist doctrine, but had a decidedly Christ-like point of view. He once preached an inspired sermon on marriage and all that it entailed. I remember him looking straight at Binky Smallwood when he said, "If you have to tell everyone you're the head of your household, then make no mistake about it, you are *not*." I have no doubt the message went straight over the fool's head.

"I taught you in Sunday School, didn't I?"

"Yes, Ma'am."

"I was rather fond of you as I recall," I said.

"Yes, Ma'am."

I said a quick prayer that this apple had rolled a good way from the tree.

"Do me a favor then, would you?" I asked.

"Yes, Ma'am?"

"Could you find Mr. Mims some tomato soup?"

"Yes, Ma'am, I could try," he responded, but did not move.

"Could you do that now, maybe?" I prodded.

"Now?" He hesitated and looked around, obviously weighing the risks of leaving me alone with Mr. Mims.

"Doesn't look to me like Mr. Mims has any fight left in him, Mr. Smallwood."

"I'm Chip, Ma'am."

"Chip. That's right. I had forgotten."

"I shouldn't leave you alone with the prisoner, Ma'am."

"Would you like to search me?"

I raised my arms. Chip backed away horrified.

"No, Ma'am, that won't be necessary."

"Run along then, Chip. I'll be fine and we'll both be here when you get back."

He hesitated, struggling I'm sure with protocol and reason. Then, taking the handcuffs from his belt, he leaned down and reached for Eddie's left arm.

"I'm sorry, Mr. Mims," he said softly as he snapped one link around Eddie's wrist and the other to the rail of the metal bed.

"Do you really think that's necessary?"

"I'll take it off when I get back," he said and let himself out of the cell without looking back.

I turned back to Eddie as soon as I heard the outer door latch shut. "Eddie, look at me," I commanded.

He moved his head slowly, almost imperceptibly, and cut his eyes toward me as he did. I moved closer to him and knelt beside his bed.

"I know you didn't do this. I'm going to get you out of here."

He didn't respond.

"Do you understand me? I'm going to get you out of here before they hurt you again."

"Don't," was all he said before he cut his eyes away again.

I wasn't one to pray often. I was raised Methodist myself and we were taught not to bother God with anything real specific, just the Lord's Prayer at night and a litany of blessings on friends and family. I looked down at the frail man who had tended my flowers with care and never asked a thing of me and I felt compelled to ask for help.

I bowed my head and spoke aloud, "Our Father, which art in heaven, hallowed be thy name. Thy kingdom come, thy will be done, on earth as it is in heaven. Give us this day our daily bread and forgive us..." My voice caught. I tried again. "Forgive us our trespasses..." I couldn't go on.

A feeble voice rose up, "As we forgive those who trespass against us."

I didn't cry at my own husband's funeral, but I cried then. And the tears didn't stop until the Public Defender arrived to meet his new client.

Eleven

Jeffrey Thatcher was a huge man who wore a stained white shirt and a crooked tie that barely reached his midriff. It may not be fair to claim that the man was disinterested. He seemed genuinely concerned that Eldred Mims was injured, but in retrospect I believe he was more worried about the impact to his career than anything else. Doing the right thing is apparently harder than it sounds when politics are involved.

He didn't want me to stay while he talked to his client, but Eddie managed to convey that he wanted me there.

"I'm Jeffrey Thatcher, Mr. Mims. You are Eldred Mims, correct?"

"Mm-hmm."

"You have a middle name, Sir?"

"Uh-uh."

"No middle name at all?"

"Uh-uh."

The entire conversation went this way. I filled in where I could, explaining about Eddie's family in Alabama and providing what little information I knew, including the general area of the woods where I thought Mr. Mims lived.

"Were you ... umm ... *home* the night Skipper Kornegay was killed, Mr. Mims? I believe that was on Thanksgiving sometime around 8:30 p.m."

"Mmm-hmm."

"Mr. Mims had Thanksgiving dinner at my house that day, Mr. Thatcher. He went home around sometime around 3 o'clock." I decided to tell the absolute truth to a point. I knew Eldred Mims hadn't killed anyone, so I clung to "the truth shall set you free" and hoped for the best. I just knew in my heart they had no evidence against him and I prayed they'd exonerate him and never solve the case. It was incredibly naive of me to even think it possible.

"Did you see or speak to anyone after you left Mrs. Beckworth's house that evening?"

"Mmm-mmm."

I was looking down and I actually remember raising my eyebrows at his answer. I knew for a fact Marcus followed him home.

"Absolutely no one? You're sure?"

"Mmm-hmm," He nodded and gave me a pointed look which Jeffrey Thatcher missed as he made notes on his legal pad.

The next few questions were a blur as I mentally raced through all the reasons why Eddie might deny the truth about Marcus. I still had not decided whether I would ask Eddie about it later when I snatched myself back to attention.

"I have to ask you about the murder itself now, Mr. Mims. Do you still want Mrs. Beckworth to stay?"

"Mmm-hmm," Eddie nodded.

"I need for you to tell me the truth, now. I'm your attorney and that means I won't repeat what I hear, unless you ask me to speak for you in court. Do you understand that?"

Eddie nodded again.

"Did you kill Skipper Kornegay, Mr. Mims?"

Eddie looked away for a moment, stared at the wall beside him as if trying to memorize something written there. He sighed once and looked back at Jeffrey Thatcher. There were unshed tears in his eyes.

"No, Sir." He shook his head and winced in pain.

"Is there any evidence, anywhere that would support or refute that claim?"

I glared at the man. Why couldn't he just put it in plain English?

"What I mean is, is there anything that would make it look like you did commit the murder, or is there anything that would prove you didn't?"

Eddie looked away again.

"No, sir," he said through clenched gums.

Chip Smallwood arrived with a cup of lukewarm soup, just as Jeffrey Thatcher was packing his ancient leather briefcase.

"I'll leave you to your supper, Mr. Mims. Here's my card if you have any questions. I'll be back in touch with you sometime tomorrow."

"Wait a minute!" I said. "What about getting him out of here?"

"And taking him where? A hospital?" Mr. Thatcher looked confused.

"Not a hospital—home!"

"Mrs. Beckworth, my client has been charged with murder. What's more, he has no home to which he can go. Even if we could get the judge to set a reasonable bail, which is highly doubtful, I don't think I could get a bondsman to post it for him. Mr. Mims will be here a while. I think you'd better get used to the idea."

"Mr. Thatcher..." My voice sounded thin, despite the heavy sarcasm in it. "Mr. Mims has been arrested for a murder he did not commit. They can't possibly keep him here under these circumstances."

"And what circumstances are you referring to, Mrs. Beckworth?"

"Any of them!" I was nearly frantic. "He's been beaten within an inch of his life, and you know as well as I do that he couldn't possibly have resisted enough to warrant these wounds. He is old and feeble and as far as I know, has never hurt a fly. I will not have him sitting in this jail waiting to be beaten again. You absolutely must do something to help him."

Jeffrey Thatcher sighed heavily and set his briefcase on the floor. He scratched the back of his neck and pushed his glasses back up on his nose.

"Common sense tells me you're probably right, Mrs. Beckworth, but the law tells me I have to go through the process it sets forth. I'll do the best I can do, but I can't make any promises. I can't even give you any hope.

"I'll be back tomorrow. Try to get some rest, Mr. Mims." With that, Mr. Thatcher gave a nod to Chip Smallwood, who unlocked the cell door and ushered him out.

Eddie took a few sips of the soup before he waved me away. I took my leave soon after. I need to make a few phone calls.

Chip Smallwood walked me to the cellblock door. I spoke quietly so Eddie would not hear.

"How's your mama and daddy doin', Chip?" I had to check a few things out before I could get where I was going with him.

He shrugged. "Not too bad, I reckon. I don't really see 'em too much."

That was a good sign.

"What a shame," I sympathized. "I thought you were pretty close to your parents."

Chip shifted uncomfortably. "Mom and me's close, I reckon. I try to see her when I can."

"You and your daddy have a fallin' out?"

My rudeness was appalling, but I pressed on anyway.

"Well, you know, fathers and sons don't always see eye to eye. I wouldn't call it a fallin' out, though."

Now, as a rule, a southern gentleman does everything he can to honor his father and mother. They could be drunken fools and you'd never hear a word against his parents. I suddenly thought of an incident from many years back, a vivid reminder of Chip's strong character.

We were finishing crafts in Sunday school one morning and I turned around just in time to see Chip Smallwood hurl a box of crayons at a boy sitting across from him. I was absolutely shocked. Chip had never given me a moment's trouble before.

I called the two boys to me and suggested that Chip apologize. I didn't think for a moment he would refuse, but that's exactly what he did. He tucked his little chin to his chest, crossed his arms, stared straight ahead and uttered not a word.

"Did you hear me, Chipper?" I asked. "I need you to apologize so we can finish up our projects."

He looked away without speaking.

"Chip, honey, I know you didn't mean to throw those crayons at C.J., so let's just say 'I'm sorry' and get it over with, okay?"

"Aw, he meant to do it all right. He was aimin' straight for my hayed, Miz Beckworth," whined C.J. McComb.

I never did get the boy to apologize, nor utter a word in his own defense. He clamped his teeth shut and refused to discuss the incident ever again. It was years before I learned that C.J. had kicked Chip under the table hard enough to leave a bruise on his shin.

Chip didn't tattle out of a sense of honor. It was clear to me now. He wouldn't rat anyone out, but he *by God* wouldn't apologize to the rat, either.

"You working the late shift tonight?"

"Yes, Ma'am, three to eleven."

"So you weren't here when they brought Mr. Mims in, huh?"

"No, Ma'am, not exactly, but they went to the infirmary first and I was here by the time they brought him to the cell."

"Did he look like that when they got him here?"

"I reckon he did. They kept him in the infirmary for quite a while."

"You think he put up that big a fight?"

"That's what they say." His leather holster crackled as he squirmed a bit and looked away.

"I know what they said. What I'm asking is, do you think he really did?" I looked him straight in the eye and he held my gaze.

"I wasn't there, Mrs. Beckworth. I really couldn't tell."

"That's what I figured you'd say," I said, resigned, but not angry.

"I'm sorry…"

I cut him off with the wave of my hand. "No need to apologize, son. Like you said, you weren't there."

He opened the outer door, walked me through it and clicked it shut.

"Chip," I said.

"Yes, Ma'am?"

"If you *had* been there, would you have let them beat him like that?"

He took a deep breath and studied his fingernails.

"No, Ma'am," he said finally, "I don't reckon I would've."

"You were a good boy, Chip Smallwood." I patted his arm. "And you're a good man."

He nodded and reached back towards the cellblock door. He pressed a button on the wall and waited to be buzzed back in.

"Keep an eye on him for me, would you?" I asked.

"I'll do my best." He nodded his head once and disappeared through the door.

I made two phone calls when I got home. The first was to Harley Odell. That is, the Honorable Harley T. Odell, Circuit Court Judge, or "Poopsie," as he was called by everyone who knew him as a child.

He punched me in the stomach when I was twelve years old and he was just ten. There was no reason for it. He just walked up to me in our back yard and punched me as hard as he could. I guess when you've been called Poopsie all your life the rage just builds up until it has to go somewhere. I threw up on his bare feet. We've never spoken of it since, but I'm almost positive Harley Odell still feels like he owes me something for his momentary cruelty.

When I told him what I knew—well, what I wanted *him* to know I knew—about Eldred Mims, he promised to look into the case and let me know what he could. He also cautioned me not to get involved in something that might be more than I bargained for.

"Too late," I said.

"Don't say another word," he warned. "I don't want to know."

"G'night, Poopsie," I said, only half-jokingly.

"Night, Ora," he growled.

The second call was to Ralph Kornegay. I hesitated before I called his home. On the one hand, I was angry over his treatment of an innocent man. On the other, he and his wife had just lost their only child. Right or wrong, I think Ralph *believed* Eldred Mims killed his son. I felt hard-pressed to stand in judgment.

I decided to tread lightly. I expressed my condolences first and my concern for Eldred Mims second. I told him I was absolutely convinced of the man's innocence and cautioned him not to jeopardize his job by losing his cool. He defended his deputies for "using appropriate force to subdue a combative suspect."

"Combative," I repeated in a dry monotone.

"Yes, Ma'am," Ralph replied, "He was combative all right."

"I find that hard to believe," I said. "The man doesn't weigh an ounce over a hundred and twenty pounds."

"I don't understand why you're defending this man, Mrs. Beckworth." His anger was evident in his use of my last name, even though we'd known each other for years.

"I'm defending him because he's innocent, Ralph."

"How about if we let a court decide that?"

"My thoughts exactly," I replied. There was a long silence on the other end of the phone.

"I'll be visiting him regularly, Ralph. If he's beaten up again, I'll make sure you're held personally responsible."

I doubt my threat worried Ralph Kornegay a bit, but at least he knew I was watching.

"Is that all?" I could hear him spitting through his teeth.

"For the time being, yes."

"Goodnight, Mrs. Beckworth."

I didn't bother to respond. I knew his phone was on its way to the receiver and the dial tone I heard confirmed that within seconds. I cradled the handset back on its perch and locked up for the night.

Twelve

I spent the next few days visiting Eldred Mims at the county jail every afternoon. His entire face was swollen, nearly beyond recognition. It was difficult for him to eat, so I took him soft food, despite the objections of the guards whose job it was to search visitors for contraband. One day it was mashed potatoes and gravy. Another day, chicken noodle soup. He especially liked Blanche's sweet potato casserole.

At some point I realized that I missed the smacking noise he usually made while talking. He held his mouth as still as possible while he ate, allowing the food to melt in his mouth before swallowing it. It made him seem like more of a stranger than he really was to me, that absence of familiar noise.

I didn't know what to say to him at first. I wanted to ask him why he lied to the lawyer, but I felt like it would take too much effort and a lot more privacy to do the subject justice.

So we talked, well … I mostly did the talking, about the weather and about the Christmas holidays coming up. We talked about what we would plant in the spring and how maybe it was time for a real garden in the back yard, a garden that grew fresh vegetables we could put up. I knew Blanche would not be thrilled with the prospect of canning, but we talked about it anyway, just like it was a sure thing. I left when it seemed he was tired of conversation. I could tell it still hurt him to speak, but every day it got easier to understand what he said. His jaw had not been broken, thank goodness, just dislocated and bruised.

He didn't seem too worried about the trial. Once when I talked to him about getting out of jail, he stopped me cold. "I'm innocent until proven guilty, Miz Beckworth. Tha's what the law says. All's I got to do is stick to the truth, way I see it. They cain't convict me of somethin' I ain't done."

I thought about it a moment and then said, "One would hope not, Mr. Mims, but then, they shouldn't have beat you up for nothing either."

"That's what I get for resistin' arrest, ain't it?"

The man had a remarkable sense of humor. Even I had to laugh at the sheer ridiculousness of it. I let the matter drop for a while.

Finally, one day when there was a disturbance at the other end of the ward, I seized the opportunity to ask him why he hadn't told Jeffrey Thatcher the truth about Marcus following him home on Thanksgiving.

"That boy didn't follow me home," Eddie said.

I felt my jaw drop in spite of my many years of instruction in good manners.

"You don't have to lie to me, Eddie," I leaned forward and whispered. "I know Marcus talked to you that evening."

"I don't know what you're talkin' about," he spoke with his jaw clinched tight and turned his head toward the wall. I couldn't let him off the hook this time.

"You most certainly do know what I'm talking about. Marcus followed you home from my house and asked you about what happened to Grace." I paused briefly and got only silence for response.

"Marcus came to my house that night. He stayed the night and left for North Carolina the next morning. I know he spoke to you because he told me he did."

Eddie turned his head slowly back toward me. "What time did he come to yo' house that night?"

"He got there about 9:30. Why?"

"He look all right to you then?"

"Eddie, if you know something I don't know, I think you'd better tell me. I know you didn't kill Skipper Kornegay, but I can't for the life of me figure out why you'd lie to your attorney about talking to Marcus when Marcus told me himself that you did."

I wasn't even sure what I expected him to say. I just knew it was odd that he'd lie about something like that.

He studied my face for a minute, like he was trying to see something in it. His dark eyes darted back and forth a couple of times and then his face went blank and he stared back at the wall.

"I thought you said you were sticking to the truth," I said quietly.

"I don't know if I can trust you, tha's all," he said, still staring at the wall.

"You can," I said, and I meant it.

He turned and looked me straight in the eye.

"I saw Marcus twice that night. Once when he came to talk to me and then later on that night when that boy chased him into the woods."

"Oh," I said and my shoulders sagged heavily. "What else did you see?"

"I didn't really see what happened," he said, his voice breaking slightly. "I just saw what was left when it was done. He musta come straight to yo' house from there."

I nodded. "He did."

"Then you know, too?"

I took a huge breath. "I do."

He looked back at the wall.

"Why haven't you said anything to the police? Or to your attorney for that matter?" I was baffled by his silence.

"I'm not really sure 'zactly why. I jes' know that Miz Blanche done been through enough this year and I cain't go bringin' no harm to her or her family. Why hadn't you told?"

"Same reason, I suppose. I just couldn't put her through it. She still doesn't know."

"I didn't figure she did," he said.

"I still don't get it, though. You could be out of this jail by now." I was genuinely puzzled.

"Miz Beckworth, with all due respect, I jus' as soon not talk about it no more. The boy done been killed and laid to rest and nothin' I can say go'n bring him back to his Mama. Tellin' about Marcus wouldn't do nothin' but bring a heap of grief onto a family what done had more'n they share already. I ain't sayin' nothin' about the boy. Not now, not ever."

Thirteen

By Christmas time, things were settling down around my house. I decided not to put up a tree at all. Walter had always climbed the pull-down attic steps to retrieve the Christmas decorations and huge artificial tree we erected each year, but neither Blanche nor I had any business trying such a thing. With all the time I had spent visiting Eddie, I hadn't had time to miss the decorations.

Every year, I gave Blanche a sizable bonus at Christmas and I made sure her family's name was on the list of Christmas charities I supported. I wanted her children to have a decent Christmas without being embarrassed or beholden to me, so I kept my benevolence at arm's length. At least, that's what I told myself I was doing. Blanche's children soon proved me wrong once again.

I remember sitting by the fire one night thinking about the holidays of the past. It was the night I finally burned Marcus's clothes, as a matter of fact. I had forgotten to call the chairman of the Needy Family program at the Baptist church to remind her about Blanche. I also had a feeling, which turned out to be accurate in the end, that my absence from the Ladies' Auxiliary over the past year would not put me in good stead with that group. I thought about buying gifts for the children myself and quickly pushed that thought aside. What did I know about buying gifts for children? I didn't know their tastes in toys or clothes, much less their sizes.

That's when I thought about the bag of clothes that was still up in my closet. Blanche had been gone for hours. There was no reason I couldn't finally rid myself, once and for all, of the evidence I'd been hiding. I put my embroidery on the lamp stand, rose from my chair and walked over to the fire, which was burning low in the grate. The black metal screen, which kept the popping embers from scorching my thick oval rug, was warm to the touch. I moved it aside, reached for the wrought iron poker hanging in its stand and nudged the glowing logs. They crackled and hissed, then settled back down to an orange glow. I left the screen where it was and went upstairs to retrieve the clothes.

I remembered washing Marcus's bloodstained pants and shirt several times before I placed them in a paper grocery sack and set them on the top shelf of my closet. So I was surprised by the strong odor that rose from the bag when I brought it down and unrolled the top. Old blood has a distinct smell, especially when it is competing with bleach and detergent.

I took the clothes downstairs and burned them, grocery bag and all. The house smelled peculiar for days, even though I sprayed Claire Burke Vapourri liberally throughout the following week. Blanche remarked on it one day.

"What's that awful smell you tryin' to cover up, Miz Ora?"

My heart nearly stopped beating.

"I think maybe a squirrel or something died in the chimney flue. It's pretty bad, isn't it?"

"You want me to call somebody 'bout it?" she asked.

"No, I don't think that's necessary. It's the holiday season; by the time we get somebody out here to check on it, the smell will have worn itself out. Let's just let it be for a few days."

"Awright," she said reluctantly. "If you say so."

I was still tiptoeing around Blanche for the most part. She managed to settle back into her routine. In fact, she seemed busier than usual, but there was something missing in her that I wasn't sure she'd ever reclaim. I missed the long, easy chats we used to have over coffee and morning chores.

A week or so before Christmas, Blanche and I were putting groceries away when I asked nonchalantly if she'd finished all her Christmas shopping.

"I ain't even started, Miz Ora," she sighed.

"What do you mean you haven't started?"

"It just don't seem like Christmas this year. I can't make myself even think about a Christmas list without my boy's name on it."

What was I thinking? I told Blanche she was off the list at the church, so gifts from them would not be forthcoming. I even gave her an extra hundred dollars to make up for the slight, but it hadn't even occurred to me that she wouldn't feel up to buying gifts for her children.

"Blanche, you can't do this."

"It's all right, Miz Ora. The girls understood when I told 'em. They said they don't feel much like celebratin' either."

"And you took that as the truth?" I demanded. "It's Christmas, Blanche!"

"You ain't got to tell me somethin' I already know."

I knew that tone. It meant Blanche would not be moved.

"I'll tell you what," I said, making my voice equally stubborn, but somehow still pleasant. "We'll have Christmas here."

Blanche protested, but I cut her off.

"Now, I know you aren't feeling up to the task and I understand why," I said using all the logic and persuasion I had learned teaching Sunday school. "But, we have to start somewhere to get your family back to normal."

Blanche just huffed and shrugged her shoulders.

"Besides, it's my first Christmas without Walter. I could really use the company." I wasn't lying when I said it, but I was a bit surprised when my heart gave a little lurch at the thought.

"That's real kind of you to say, Miz Ora, but I know you just being nice. You ain't complained once about being by yourself."

"Well, just because I haven't complained doesn't mean I haven't felt it, Blanche. I'm serious. I want you and the girls here for Christmas. I want a huge tree and decorations and lots of presents under the tree. It's not just my first Christmas without Walter. It's the first time I haven't been involved in all the charities and holiday functions we did together."

"Y'all sho' did do a lot of charity. I been wondering why you ain't still involved in all that." Blanche was not being intrusive, just candid.

I pulled a couple of packets of Earl Grey tea from the pantry, and then busied myself putting water in the kettle and heating it on the stove. Blanche took two teacups down from the cabinet, opened the packets I had left on the counter and hung the teabags over the edge of the cups. We were quite a team, I thought. One starts a task and the other finishes without a word being spoken.

I turned to face her and put my hands on my hips. "To tell the truth, I hadn't thought past my relief at being freed of the obligation. It's not that I didn't enjoy the work Walter and I did. I guess it's just that I never felt like I had a choice in the matter."

"I know just what you mean," Blanche said under her breath.

"But I do have a choice now, and I would love for you and your children to spend Christmas with me this year."

"You ain't got to do this, Miz Ora." I could tell Blanche was softening.

"I'm well aware of that," I replied.

"I just don't think I'm up to it is all."

"Well, you think about it and let me know," I said reasonably. "In the meantime, I'm going to get the girls to get my tree down from the attic. Even if they don't have any presents, I think it will be good for them to help me decorate my house."

"Yes, Ma'am, I think they'll like that a lot," Blanche said.

The whistle sounded on the teakettle and we dropped the conversation as we had our tea together.

Fourteen

Just after lunch, I made an excuse to call another taxi to pick me up. If Blanche was suspicious, she didn't let on. I gave instructions to the driver to take me to an address on Canal Street and he silently drove me there. I asked him to wait and he did as I walked up the clean-swept, but cracked and broken sidewalk to the front porch. I'd seen Blanche's house before, but I had never been inside. I was raising my hand to knock on the door when it was opened by a young man I guessed to be around twenty years old. I couldn't say which of us were more surprised, but I found my voice first.

"Is Patrice home?" I asked.

"Uh, yes ma'am, she's, um, in the bathroom right now," he stammered.

"And you would be...?" I fished for a name.

"Um, late, actually."

"Well, that's not what I meant, but I'll bite. Late for what?"

"For work," he replied as he tried to angle his muscular body around my slight one.

"Hold on there a minute," I told him as I blocked his path with my left hand. "Who are you and what are you doing here?" I didn't add "alone with Patrice", but you can bet I was thinking it.

"I'm a friend of Patrice's. I was just visiting with her before work and I'm really late right now, Ma'am." He kept his tone polite, but I could tell it was all he could manage.

I heard Patrice's voice before she appeared in the doorway. "Who're you talkin' to, Cedric?" She stopped short when she saw me through the space between his arm and the door jam. "Mrs. Beckworth! What are you...? Why...? Is something...? Is everything okay?" She finally managed to ask.

"Everything is fine at my house, but perhaps I should be asking you that question."

"Oh," Patrice paused. "Oh, yes, everything's fine. Cedric was just helping me study for a Latin test."

"Quota hora est?" I asked, looking straight at the young man.

"Say what?" Cedric sputtered.

I could see Patrice's shoulders fall as he failed my impromptu exam.

"Studying Latin are you?" I intoned drily.

"Go on to work, Cedric," Patrice sighed.

"And don't come back," I added.

"No problem," he said as he abruptly dropped his respectful tone. "Later, Patrice," he threw over his shoulder as he slid around me.

"About two years later or she's jailbait," I threw right back.

He grunted and broke into a jog as he stepped off the porch and headed down the sidewalk.

I turned my attention back to Patrice.

"Would you like to come in?" Patrice asked softly.

"Actually, I was hoping I could get you to come shopping with me. The taxi is waiting."

"Does Mama know you're here?" I knew what she was asking.

"No, it was supposed to be a surprise. Turns out it is *quite* a surprise."

"It's not what you think, Mrs. Beckworth," she protested.

"Oh?" was all I said.

"I'll get my coat," she said and opened the door wider to usher me inside.

I stepped into the living room of Blanche's small frame house and was struck by the darkness of it. The inside walls were covered with wood paneling. A large brown gas heater burned noisily at one end of the room and a picture of The Last Supper hung wearily over a deep red couch at the other end. I studied the picture as I waited for Patrice to reappear from the door of what I presumed was her bedroom.

The scene was the same as I had seen it in numerous churches and homes over the years. A green-walled room surrounded a long table around which Christ's disciples gathered, their attention focused on the robed man gesturing from the center of the table. The man's hair was long and wavy as I had seen depicted in many paintings and renderings of Jesus. The biggest difference was in his skin-tone, which was four shades darker than any I had ever seen.

If Patrice noticed me staring when she emerged from her room, she did not acknowledge it.

"Are you ready?" I asked.

"Yes, Ma'am," she replied. "Where are we going?"

"Christmas shopping," I said with a lightness I did not feel at the moment.

Patrice and I slid into the back seat of the taxi and I asked him to take us to the J.C. Penney store downtown.

"Meter's been running," he said as he pulled away from the curb.

I ignored the comment and turned toward Patrice.

"Tell me about this young man ... what was his name? Sidney?"

"Cedric," she sighed. "What do you want to know?"

"How old is he?"

"Twenty-one," she answered.

"Does your mama know about him?"

"She's known Cedric since he was a baby!" Patrice sounded a bit defensive.

"I didn't ask if she knew *him*; I asked if she knew *about* him. There's a difference."

"What about him?" I was surprised at how well this sixteen year old child could deflect questions.

"Well, for starters, why is he visiting you without your mama being home? Does she know about that?"

"No, ma'am," Patrice groaned.

"Do you think she would approve?"

"No, ma'am." She was near tears now. "Are you going to tell her?"

"I don't like to lie to your mother." The irony of my phrasing was not lost on me.

"She'll kill me for lettin' him in the house when she isn't there."

"Patrice," I sighed, "You're a bright girl. Exceptionally bright from all I know. Do you realize the chances you're taking with your life?"

"We were just hanging out together, Miz Beckworth! Honest, we weren't doing anything wrong!"

"If your mama doesn't know about it, it's wrong. What I'm worried about is what *you* don't know."

"I know he likes me," she said defensively. "He thinks I'm smart and mature..." She paused and then added, "and pretty, too."

"Lot of people think those things about you," I agreed. "But not all of them want the same thing from you as he does."

"How do you know what he wants?" she asked, suddenly sullen, as if she knew very well what I was going to say.

"Because I know, that's how."

Patrice sighed and slumped into the corner of the back seat.

"Patrice, you have promise. Do you understand that? You have the talent and intelligence to break free of your situation and make something of yourself."

She rolled her eyes and turned her head toward the window.

"Something much more than just a young single mother, or a wife if you're lucky."

"Bible says being a wife is a good thing," Patrice countered with the only argument she could find.

"It is a good thing—at the right time and under the right circumstances. Otherwise, it can wind up being a life sentence."

"You didn't have it so bad, did you?"

"I wasn't having sex at sixteen."

That got her attention. Patrice sat up straight and looked me right in the eye.

"I never did, Miz Beckworth! *Never!*"

"Good!" I beamed. "And I'm going to help you keep it that way!"

She sat completely still, staring now at the back of the driver's seat.

"Are you gonna tell Mama?" A single tear escaped the eyes that had long been full and threatening to overflow.

"No, I'm not," I replied.

"What are you going to do, then?"

"I'm not sure just yet. We'll have to wait and see."

Just then, the taxi pulled up in front of the two-story J.C. Penney building three blocks from my house. I could see the twins and Gracie getting off the bus and racing toward my front porch. They never looked in our direction as I paid the cab driver.

"Let's go, Patrice," I said jovially as I took her arm and guided her into the square beige building. "We've got a lot of shopping to do and only a little time to do it."

We climbed the marble stairs to the children's department and found plenty of clothes from which to choose. Patrice knew all the new styles and the sizes the younger girls wore. We chose a dress for each of them, with matching lace socks and patent leather shoes. I thought the socks might be a bit too childish for the twins, but Patrice assured me they would be good for church functions.

We bought smock tops and two pairs of jeans for each of them, and completed our shopping with fancy new underwear from the children's department.

Then we headed back down the wide staircase to the Misses' section. I knew Blanche's size from purchasing uniforms over the years. Patrice and I found a bright blue suit and a matching wide-brimmed hat for Blanche to wear to church. Afterwards, I chose two house dresses and a pair of soft white slippers that I thought Blanche would enjoy.

Once that was done, I ushered Patrice to the Junior Department and told her to start trying on clothes.

"For me?" she asked, her eyes glistening with unshed tears.

"Of course, for you!" I laughed. "What? Did you think you weren't included in Christmas?"

"I thought maybe you were mad at me," Patrice said shyly.

"Don't mistake concern for anger, child. I care about you and I care about your mother and I can't stand the thought of her bearing anymore heartbreak."

With that, the tears spilled over in her eyes and she brushed them away with the back of her hands.

"Okay, no crying allowed," I said, and pushed her toward the clothes. "Let's see how some of these things look on you."

I took my initial purchases back to the service department to be gift-wrapped. When I returned, I found a chair near the dressing rooms and let Patrice model every outfit she liked, which turned out to be a considerable few. I paid careful attention to sizes and favorites and, when we were done, sent Patrice to the back to collect our wrapped goods. I chose three pairs of slacks, two shirts and a dress that Patrice had adored, even though I thought it a bit too short for my standards. After paying the clerk for them, I asked her to have them wrapped and told her I would pick them up later.

I didn't want Patrice to see what I had purchased, so I had the clerk take the other items away from the register, thinking Patrice would return any moment. When she didn't, I headed for the service department. She wasn't there, either, and the clerk I had originally seen had been replaced by a middle-aged woman whose thin lips were flanked by the lines of a perpetual scowl.

I identified myself and asked for my packages.

"Oh, Mrs. Beckworth," the clerk gushed, "I'm so glad you're here! I just had the most unpleasant experience with a Negro girl over your packages."

I must have been stunned, because it didn't register with me what she meant.

"What happened? Did she pick up my gifts?"

"Oh, of course not," the clerk said confidently. "There is no way in the world I would let one of those people steal your things."

"Steal my things?" It took hindsight to realize that the sinking feeling in my chest hit before I truly understood what she was saying.

"Why, a girl was *just here*, trying to take your gifts. I turned her away, of course. She wasn't going to pull anything over on me!"

"Where is she?" I demanded.

I suppose she thought my anger was directed at the object of her scorn because she nearly crowed in triumph, "Why, the manager has her in his office right now. I imagine he's searched her and…"

I didn't stay to hear the rest. I headed right for Red Bascomb's office, which was just three doors down. I didn't bother to knock.

"Patrice!" I called her name even as I was turning the knob. I saw Bascomb's back before I saw the frightened child huddled against the wall. He whirled to face me and she inched from behind him and ran straight into my arms.

I held her against my shoulder and did my best to comfort her, all the while glaring at the stunned man in front of me.

"What is the meaning of this?" I demanded of him.

"Why I was just… I was told…" Red Bascomb faltered. "Is she with you?" he finally managed.

"Looks like it, doesn't it," I said through clenched teeth.

"I think I've made a mistake, Ora," Red Bascomb admitted.

"What gave it away, Red?"

To his credit he had the decency to blush.

"I was told she was attempting to collect items that didn't belong to her," Red stammered in his defense.

"She was with *me*!" I hissed.

"I see that now," he said, his composure nearly regained, "and I certainly apologize. But, it was an honest mistake. I truly didn't know, Ora."

I actually stamped my foot at him. Then I took Patrice by the shoulders and turned her sodden face towards him.

"Tell *her* that."

Red let out a sigh. "I *am* sorry, Miss Lowery. I hope you will forgive me, but I didn't realize who you were."

Patrice just nodded and turned away. Then, bless her heart, that child drew herself up to her full height and walked serenely from Red's office and through the store. I followed as she stopped at the service desk and faced the clerk.

"I've come to collect Miz Beckworth's packages," she said to the bewildered woman, who simply stood with her scowling mouth hanging wide open.

I slapped my hand down on the counter, my bracelets jingling noisily. "Did you hear her?" I asked.

The clerk fumbled with several large bags behind the counter and eventually handed them to Patrice, who took them in each hand and proceeded through the store. Apparently the grapevine was short there, because every clerk in the store stopped what they were doing and watched that child pass with head held high and tears nearly dried.

I wish I could say that I fully comprehended what took place that day, but it is only in the retelling of the story that I understand my part in it. And, Lord forgive me, I just now realized how much my indignation was misplaced. I was upset that Patrice had been treated badly; there's no doubt about that. But, it never dawned on me how wrong it was that I tied her innocence to the fact that she was with me, not who she was, and I am humbled by my ignorance.

Fifteen

The girls had a ball retrieving my decorations from the attic that night after supper. In fact, they found a good bit more than just decorations. It had been years since I had climbed the narrow steps to my attic, but the girls would not have it but that I join them there to see the treasures they had found.

A cedar chest full of my grandmother's old clothes and my mother's wedding dress lay in one corner. One box held a variety of crocheted doilies and embroidered handkerchiefs and other various tablecloths and linens. There was an entire stack of hatboxes and a hall tree sporting a half dozen more hats on its hooks. Another box held scrapbooks full of pictures dating to the late 1800s. My wedding album was there and I sat down at my mother's old dressing table to look through the evidence of my innocent hope. In one picture, I sat in an ornate chair, smiling up over my shoulder at Walter with an expression of unabashed adoration on my face. He was returning my gaze with a beguiled grin of his own.

Funny, I hadn't remembered adoring Walter like that. Nor did I remember him ever being particularly captivated by me. As I sat there in my attic, with three little girls busily rooting through and trying on various costumes of another era, I wondered if time had so altered my memory that I had forgotten such things as love, or if pictures did indeed tell the story.

I finally dragged the girls away from their plunder by promising hot chocolate while we decorated the tree. I also assured them we'd return to the attic to play at some later date.

Patrice, sufficiently recovered from the afternoon trauma, washed the dishes and made the cocoa while Blanche rested in Walter's recliner and watched our festive doings. Blanche would normally have gone home much earlier, but it was Friday and the girls wouldn't have to go to school the next day, so we were all carried away with our merriment.

Before we knew it, the clock chimed eleven times and we looked at each other in amazement. Blanche was snoring softly from the chair and Grace had fallen asleep on the couch, but the rest of us were still going strong when we put on the last ornament, a brightly lit angel to adorn the treetop.

I sent the twins to the guest bedroom and Patrice to Walter's old room, which hadn't been used once since his death. Blanche kept it clean and changed the sheets every couple of weeks, but I had scarcely opened the door in the past year.

I couldn't remember exactly when or why Walter had moved out of our room and into what used to be the guest room. Something about his snoring disturbing my sleep … or my restlessness disturbing his. I can't remember which came first. One day he moved to the extra bed in the middle of the night. Then he moved his clothes from our closet so that he wouldn't wake me up when he got ready for work. Eventually we started calling it his room, which necessitated the decoration of my old sewing room as the new guest room.

Patrice was just happy to have a bed to fall into after her long, long day. I took blankets down to cover Grace and Blanche, turned off the tree lights, locked all the doors and returned to Patrice's room to check on her before retiring myself. She was buried in the covers with pillows piled high under her head.

"You comfortable?" I asked, knowing the answer already.

"This is the best bed I ever slept in, Miz Beckworth. I slept at my friend's house a couple of times, but I've never slept anywhere all by myself."

"Never?"

"No'm, not ever once."

"You don't have your own room now?" I asked.

"There's only two bedrooms in our house. One's got two twin beds and Mama just has a double."

"Goodness, that's not many beds for all you children! How do you manage?" I couldn't seem to help being nosy.

"Well, me and Gracie sleep in one bed and the twins in the other. Marcus used to sleep on the sofa when he was home or, every once in a while, with Mama. I guess I could sleep on the sofa if I wanted to sleep by myself, but it just doesn't seem right somehow."

"You miss your brother, don't you?"

"Yes, Ma'am, I do sometimes. Long as I just pretend he's away at boot camp I do pretty good. I can't hardly look at a semi truck now, though. It makes me remember too much."

"I'm sorry about that, Patrice."

"Nothin' for you to be sorry 'bout, Miz Beckworth. You didn't do nothin' wrong."

"Anything wrong," I replied. I can't for the life of me figure out why correcting her grammar seemed like the thing to do at the time.

"Yes, Ma'am," she smiled sheepishly.

"You sleep tight now, okay?"

"I will," Patrice murmured sleepily. "Real tight in this comfy ol' bed." She turned away from me then, rolling to her right side.

"I sure am sorry about what happened today," I said gently.

She turned her head back to look at me with calm acceptance. "Oh, it's all right, Miz Beckworth. I'm kind of used to it by now."

Her reply stung me worse than the horror we faced in the department store, because she told the pure truth of it.

Sixteen

The next day, after Blanche and the girls had eaten breakfast and gone on home, I walked down to the Woolworth store to buy stockings and little gifts for Blanche's girls. I had an awful lot of fun choosing perfumes and bath oils and shiny hair clips for each of them. And I bought Blanche a big box of chocolate turtles, which I knew were her favorites.

I had just finished making all my purchases and was about to head for home when I saw a rack of bicycles in the front window of the store. I somehow missed them on my way in and they were marked for clearance, it being so close to Christmas Eve.

They had ten-speeds in every color and size, and smaller bikes with banana seats and tassels hanging from the handlebars. I thought about Blanche and her girls walking everywhere and, although I couldn't imagine Blanche heaving her ample behind onto a bicycle of *any* shape or size, I thought it might be good for the girls to be a bit more mobile.

I stood there contemplating the purchase of four bicycles and how much it would cost, sale or no sale. I had almost talked myself out of spending the money when a something occurred to me that stopped me in my tracks. What if Grace had ridden a bicycle to my house the day that Skipper Kornegay had stopped her in the woods?

I bought four bicycles. The largest was for Patrice, a 21 inch yellow ten-speed with curved handlebars like the racers use. Two smaller ten-speeds were perfect for the twins, just alike except that one was bright orange and the other purple.

I bought a pink bike for Gracie, with a white basket in front and glittery plastic tassels hanging from the handlebars. It was the perfect size for her, big enough that she could ride without the training wheels that were attached, but small enough that they came with it. I had no idea whether any of the girls could ride the bicycles, but I sure felt better once I bought them. I arranged to have them delivered on Christmas Eve. I would put them in the garage until Christmas morning.

I stopped at the soda counter after I made my purchases. I had intended to go home to have lunch, but I thought of the hot dogs on grilled buns Walter and I used to enjoy there on Saturdays. And cherry cokes. Real cherry coke, not the store-bought canned ones you get today. I sat at the counter, feeling shaky and unladylike on the wobbly stool, but I stayed right there. I ate my hotdog with plenty of mustard and relish and I felt right proud of myself for all I'd accomplished in one morning.

I walked home after that, feeling more full than proud. A stiff wind had kicked up and I had to lean into it to keep from being blown off my feet. It didn't help that my bags full of whatnots for the girls kept filling with air and pulling me backward like parachutes. I stopped and tied them closed with the handles. Then I leaned forward and pushed on toward home.

I was almost home when I got to thinking how silly I must look, all ninety-eight pounds of me, buckin' a headwind. It just tickled me so much that I got to giggling. Inside at first, but then it just bubbled out the top and I was nearly crying with laughter by the time I hit my porch. I had been so focused on putting one foot in front of the other that I hadn't looked up yet when I set my foot on the first step.

"'Bout time you got home," a voice boomed from my porch. I looked up, choking back a giggle.

"Whatcha' laughin' at, Ora Lee?" the Honorable Harley T. Odell thundered from his seat in one of my rockers.

Harley Odell was as large as I was slight, with a bulging belly that stretched the hope of any wrinkle right out of his expensive western-cut shirt. He sat with one foot propped on the runner of the chair and his snakeskin boots gleamed shiny gray beneath the dark blue slacks he wore. His face was covered in a neatly-trimmed, but thick beard of more salt than pepper. A handlebar mustache, waxed and twisted in place just so, covered his top lip and provided a frame for his bulbous red nose. He looked like a cross between Santa and his lead reindeer with a little John Wayne thrown in for good measure.

I hiccupped through the last of my giggles, set my packages on the top step and stared at my visitor with both arms akimbo.

"Well, if it ain't Poopsie, it's the devil himself!"

"Afternoon, Ora Lee."

Lord, but the man had a voice as smooth as silk, even if it was a few decibels above normal.

"I wasn't expecting company or I'da been here to meet you."

"I woulda called," he drawled, "but I didn't think of stopping here until I was coming through town."

"How long you been waiting?"

"Oh, 'bout thirty minutes or so. It's nice on this porch. Warm for December, wind and all."

"That's a long time, nice porch or not. What brings you here, Poopsie?"

"A strong desire to lose that old nickname, for one," he said with a wry smile.

"Aw, I always thought it suited you just fine. Would you like some tea?"

"You haven't changed a whit since high school, Ora Lee. Still got that sharp tongue, tempered only by your earnest devotion to the social graces. Sweet, please."

I gathered my packages without a word and was soon back with two glasses of sweet tea. I settled into my chair and sipped the icy brew.

"You didn't finish answering my question. What can I do for you?"

"Glad you asked." Harley Odell leaned forward as he spoke. "I got a problem over at the jail I was hoping you could help me with."

"What kind of problem?"

"Got an old man there I'm pretty sure didn't do what the sheriff says he did and I don't know how to handle it."

"Eldred Mims?"

"The one and only."

"What gave it away?" I huffed. "I told you myself he couldn't have killed anyone."

"Yep, you did. And I'm inclined to believe you. Problem is, I've got to do something with the man between now and time for the trial. I'm thinking of letting him out on bail, but nobody'll post it without him having an address, much less a home."

"I can vouch for him, if that's what you're asking," I said.

"Well, in a way, I am," Harley squirmed in the rocker, "but there's more to it than that."

"Such as?"

"You visit him fairly often, don't you?"

"Much as I can, yes."

"I'm just wondering why it is you do that." Harley cocked his head sideways and peered at me curiously.

"'Cause of what you just said. I think Ralph Kornegay's got the wrong man and I feel bad for him, being in jail like that. And I think the longer he stays there, the more likely it is he'll be hurt worse than he was already hurt."

"How bad do you want him out?" Harley asked, leaning forward again. "Or maybe I should rephrase that. How much are you willing to bet he didn't do it?"

"How much is his bail?"

"I haven't set it yet. Hearing's Monday afternoon."

I was getting tired of the game, but I decided to hang in a while longer. "How much are you thinking?"

"Normally, it'd have to be a hundred thousand or more, but I'd be willing to make a deal for less."

"Get to the point, Poopsie."

"Fifty thousand and you never call me Poopsie again."

"Done," I said, thinking I had gotten off quite easily.

Harley Odell reached down and snagged his hat from where it lay on the floor beside the chair. Then, rocking forward for momentum, he heaved his massive frame to a standing position and paused for a moment in front of me. He seemed to be considering something carefully.

"I'll have my secretary call you Monday. She'll have all the details on posting Mr. Mims' bail."

"That will be fine, Harley," I said, "and I appreciate what you're doing for the man."

"Well, I'm not sure how much you gonna appreciate the rest of the deal, but I really have no choice."

"The rest of the deal?"

"Get your guest room ready, Ora. He'll be staying with you."

I was too stunned to speak and ol' Poopsie was apparently counting on that. He tipped his hat and strode off my porch with surprising agility for a man his size. He was in his car and backing down my driveway before I found my voice. There was no one there to hear me talking to myself.

"Well, my Lord, Ora. What have you gotten yourself into now?"

Seventeen

Clara Jean Munderson called me at 10:00 sharp on Monday morning. I was sitting at the kitchen table updating my Christmas list for next year when the phone rang.

"Mornin', Mrs. Beckworth," a soft, pleasant drawl greeted me. "This is Clara Munderson at Judge Odell's office."

"Yes, Clara Jean, I recognized your voice," I responded affably.

Another of my Sunday School members, the only child of Clarice and Bill Munderson was the consummate professional. Never one to play noisily with the others in her class, Clara Jean was always amiable, always respectful, but not in the least a pushover. It was amazing how she had handled herself as a child and how that translated into the position she had held for the past twenty years. She was gentle and compassionate and a good listener, which led many of her friends to confide in her on a regular basis. And she'd have died before she ever broke a confidence.

I was on the Baptist Women's Prayer Chain for many years before I got kicked off for telling them to stop using God as an excuse to gossip. I can assure you, if Clara Jean ever betrayed a word of what went on behind Harley Odell's closed door, I'd have heard about it. And if the door was closed, it stayed closed. God Himself wouldn't get through to the judge if He didn't have special clearance or an appointment. Clara Jean never married, leading half the self-righteous old biddies on the chain to speculate that she was keeping far more than Poopsie's professional business a secret. I knew better than to contemplate such a thing. The thought of ol' Poopsie in the throes of passion was just more than I could stand.

"Judge Odell wanted me to give you some information about posting bail for Mr. Eldred Mims. You have something to write with?"

"Matter of fact, I do, Clara Jean. Go ahead."

I took her instructions carefully, repeating them back to her to make sure I had them straight. I could hear Blanche go quiet at the kitchen sink. It's funny how I did not notice the noise of dishes being washed and the low wordless tunes Blanche hummed until both were abruptly stopped. As I finished my call and hung up, Blanche sat down at the table, drying her hands on the dish towel that hung from the waistband of her wide apron.

"What's goin' on with Mr. Mims?" Blanche could be downright blunt when she wanted to know something.

"Well, I was going to tell you about that this morning," I replied, in no real hurry to do the telling. I braced myself for her reaction and dove right in.

"I'm posting bail for Eddie tomorrow morning."

"You go'n do what?" Blanche exploded.

"I'm getting Eddie out of jail," I repeated.

"I heard what you said," Blanche replied. "What I want to know is what in the world you think you're doing!"

"I'm helping a friend is what I'm doing," I looked her dead in the eye and silently dared her to argue with that. Apparently dares didn't worry Blanche one little bit.

"Eldred Mims ain't no friend of yours, Miz Ora, and you know that plain and true. Now I want you to tell me what is goin' on here."

I stood then and pulled myself up to my full five feet plus three very short inches.

"I am posting bail for Mr. Mims tomorrow morning, after which he will be staying in Walter's old room. If you have a problem with that, I'll be happy to get the room ready myself. Otherwise, I don't want to hear another word about it."

I turned my back on Blanche then and left the room. I could still hear her muttering as I went upstairs to do some paperwork. Bravado aside, I planned to stay out of her way as much as I could that day.

The next morning I stopped by Citizen's Family Bank and picked up a Cashier's Check for $50,000, as Clara Jean had instructed. The head teller was Seeley Graves. She'd been at the bank for ten years and was the president of the Junior Woman's Club. I knew her well enough to know she was a gossip of epic proportions. Seeley repeated the information I gave her with a quizzical arch of one perfectly plucked eyebrow.

"It's none of your business, Seeley," I said without humor. "Just cut the check and quit wondering."

She sniffed disapprovingly, but presented me with the requested instrument in good time.

"Is there anything else I can help you with, Mrs. Beckworth?" Her sincerity was overwhelming.

"As a matter of fact, yes, there is." I looked her straight in the eye. "You can remember the confidential nature of this transaction and keep it to yourself."

I slipped the check into my pocketbook and snapped it shut. Then I smiled sweetly at her, but narrowed my eyes and said pointedly, "If I hear one word that even makes me *think* a mutual acquaintance knows my personal business, I'll be on Steve Haskins' doorstep so fast it'll make your head spin."

Walter had been on the board of directors at the bank and a frequent golfing partner of the bank president. Seeley knew it was no empty threat.

I knew I was being a bit touchy about the matter, but I felt no regret at my pre-emptive behavior. The older I get, the less I care what people think of me, but I care a great deal about people knowing my business.

I arrived at the Clerk's office promptly at 10:00 a.m., paid the bail and signed the prerequisite documents. Then I took the stairs to Judge Owen's office on the third floor of the courthouse. Clara Jean was at the coffee pot when I walked through the door. Either someone tipped her off as to my arrival or she simply counted on my punctuality, because she had an extra cup already poured and in her hand.

"Good morning, Mrs. Beckworth," she smiled with genuine hospitality and grace. "Cream and sugar, right?"

I was impressed. "Thank you, Clara Jean." I smiled and took the proffered mug.

"Judge Odell would like to speak with you personally," she continued. "Do you have a few minutes?"

"I'm in no hurry," I replied.

She returned to her desk and sat, moving a stack of files to the right, out of her way and out of my sight.

"You all ready for Christmas?" she asked pleasantly.

"Just about," I answered. "I'm having some company this year."

"Oh, I know," she said quickly. "Judge Odell filled me in. I hope you don't mind."

"You mean Mr. Mims," I said. "Yes, he'll be staying with me, too, but I was referring to Blanche and her children. I've invited them to have Christmas with me."

"Oh, I didn't realize," she blurted. "Why, that's quite a houseful, isn't it?"

She meant nothing by it, I knew, but the incident with Patrice had put me on alert for bigotry of any kind.

"My house has been empty for years. It will be nice to fill it with family," I said, trying not to sound snippy, but not succeeding.

"Of course it will," she smiled. "Mr. Beckworth hasn't been gone that long. I know how hard it is to be alone sometimes."

And she did know. I instantly regretted my wariness. Clara Jean came along late in her parents' lives. Clarice died of breast cancer several years prior and her father had a stroke less than a year afterward. The last I had heard he was still languishing in a nursing home nearby. Sometimes I could just cut my tongue out.

"We would love to have you join us, Clara Jean," I said gently. "We'll be having a big dinner Christmas Eve."

"Oh, thank you for asking, Mrs. Beckworth, but..."

"I understand completely," I said.

"No, no..." she trailed off again. "It's just that ... I haven't really told anyone yet."

She looked over her shoulder at the closed door behind her. I braced myself for the confession of the century.

"I may have a date Christmas Eve." I swear she giggled.

"A date!" I can be a little too loud when I'm caught off guard.

"Shhhh..." Clara Jean warned, nodding toward the closed door behind her. "He doesn't know yet."

"Why would he care?" Lord, I'm nosy.

She looked over her shoulder again and whispered loud enough for me to hear, "I don't want him to worry."

"Poopsie? Worried?"

"Mrs. Beckworth, I have strict orders to correct you every time you call him that." Ever on guard, that girl is.

"You know about our deal then." I shrugged. "Am I allowed to call him Harley?"

"You and you alone," She said with an amused grin. "Judge Odell has been like a father to me. I don't want him to know about my date until I see where it's going."

That little bit of information put to rest any of the rumors I had ever heard.

I got the feeling Clara Jean wanted to tell someone her news. I suddenly felt maternal. "Well, he won't hear it from me. Anything else you want to share about this mystery man? I'm all ears and no mouth where you are concerned."

"Well, I've known him all my life, but I hadn't seen him in years. I ran into him when I took some papers over to the jail the other day. We got to talking about Christmas and how neither of us had plans, and I'm not sure who even asked who, but suddenly we had a date for Christmas Eve!"

I reached out and put my hand on hers. "Clara Jean, I couldn't be happier for you. I hope you have the merriest Christmas ever."

Just then the door flew open and Harley Odell appeared, taking far more than his share of space in the room, as usual.

"Well, if it isn't the ever-punctual Ora Lee," the honorable judge boomed. "You ready to take care of this business?"

"Ready as I'll ever be," I allowed with more than a hint of resignation.

"Well, come on in and we'll go over a few details before I release Mr. Mims."

I followed him into his office and sat in one of the huge leather wing chairs in front of his desk.

"I'll get right to the point," Harley said, more quietly than I anticipated. "Is there anything else I should know about Eldred Mims before I place him in your care?"

"Can't think of a thing," I said calmly.

He leaned back then, his massive chair groaning loudly from the shifting weight. Folding his arms across his chest he eyed me curiously through his bifocals.

"Nary a thing, eh?" I swear he smirked then and I hated him for it.

"I don't have time for games, Poopsie," I snapped.

"Uh, uh, uh!" he half-grinned. "A deal's a deal."

"Old habits die hard," I grumbled. "I have no idea what you want me to say, *Judge Odell!* He's a harmless old man who more than likely was in the wrong place at the wrong time. Either release him to me or let me go get my check back to the bank before I lose a day's interest on it."

"Something's not right here, Ora Lee, and I'd be willing to bet my life on that one. But, seeing as how you aren't talking, I'll have to just trust my gut and keep an eye out for trouble."

"I don't think there will be any trouble, Harley. He's just an old man," I repeated with just a hint more desperation than conviction.

"I'll have Chip Smallwood bring him by your house this evening after dark. I don't expect any trouble out of Ralph or his deputies; I've made sure they know who's watching them at this point."

I nodded once in reply.

"I doubt you'll have any trouble from the townspeople, but I wouldn't be advertising the fact that he's staying there if I were you."

"Hell, they didn't like it when I was having him mow my yard. Dovey Kincaid will broadcast it the minute she figures it out, and I know that won't take long."

"Are you sure you're up to this?" Poopsie sounded concerned this time.

"I'm sure," I said softly. "Besides, I still have Blanche to help me."

"She's a good woman, that maid of yours."

"She's my friend," I said and then repeated, "my friend."

"As am I," Harley said, more gently than I'd ever heard him be.

Eddie arrived that afternoon. I watched Chip walk him up my front walk, one hand holding the old man's elbow, the other carrying a paper sack which turned out to be the sum total of Eddie's earthly possessions.

Blanche helped me deposit him in Walter's old room. He looked decidedly out of place in it, uncomfortable even. He looked around for a place to put his hat and then, finding nothing he deemed suitable, folded it in half and tucked in his back pocket.

"I hope you'll be comfortable here, Eddie," I said, absurdly. The man had been sleeping in a jail cell for weeks and outside for who knows how long.

"Yes'm, I reckon I'll be fine," he nodded.

"Is there anything I can get for you?" I asked, ever the hostess.

"No'm, I'm all right," he mumbled and fidgeted quietly. "'Cept..."

"Except what?" I asked.

"I wonder could you show me where's the toilet?" he asked.

"Oh!" I blushed furiously. "It's down the hall on the right."

He nodded and rocked back and forth on his feet.

"I'm going to put on a pot of tea while you get settled," I said and left the room quickly.

Blanche had dinner warming in the oven when she left an hour later and Eddie and I took our first meal together in the formal dining room. We sat at opposite ends of the long mahogany table that had once belonged to my mother. Neither of us spoke much. I assume that Eddie felt the same discomfort I did, but I doubt he was thinking the same thing, that the table itself seemed like a river of blood between us. We took all our future meals at the kitchen table.

I had no fewer than twenty calls that week about my harboring a criminal. If they knew who the real criminal was, they'd have called the sheriff isntead. Eddie made himself scarce every time the phone rang.

Funny that none of them showed up on my doorstep like I expected. I guess they truly were afraid of Eddie, as unlikely as it seemed to me. But they didn't know what I knew, so in a way I could understand. I handled the calls as best I could, assuring each caller that I would not be foolish enough to open my home to the man if I had any doubt whatsoever about his innocence. Nothing seemed to make a difference to any of them, though, and eventually I stopped answering the telephone.

I briefly entertained the thought that a few of the townsmen might show up at my door with shotguns and ropes in hand, but I soon chided myself for imagining such drama.

Eighteen

School was out the week before Christmas and Blanche's girls were giddy with excitement. Even Blanche managed to suppress her sadness enough to get into the spirit of the season. I think it was hard not to anticipate the opening of all the presents under our tree. The three younger children spent most of their time with us, but Patrice had taken part-time job as a cashier at Winn Dixie and worked most evenings.

It's funny how, just when you think you've settled into a routine and you know what to expect, something seemingly insignificant becomes a revelation.

We decided to bake cookies, a task I previously thought to be a necessary, but not particularly heartwarming, part of the holiday routine. I had always helped Blanche by planning, shopping and organizing before the cookies were baked, and by packing and sorting for the various charities afterwards. That was before we had children in the house.

Knowing I had resigned from most of my civic duties, Blanche assumed we would omit the baking part of our routine when she asked about the cookies one night at the dinner table.

"I don't reckon we go'n be bakin' them Christmas cookies this year, 'less you got something I don't know about."

Three little heads snapped to attention and the younger girls all spoke at once.

"Cookies?"

"Aw, I done said it now," moaned Blanche.

"I'll help, Mama," Patrice said, more eager than resigned.

"Pleeeease…" came the chorus.

"I don't see why not," I said and Blanche smiled in spite of herself.

We decided to make Christmas Butter Cookies, so the girls could use the cookie cutters and sprinkles, and Lemon Squares, Blanche's favorite. Then I said I'd add Bourbon Balls to the menu. They were easy to make and required no baking at all, so I thought I could handle those myself while the girls decorated their cookies.

"Bourbon Balls?" Blanche asked. "We entertainin' this year?"

"Not on a grand scale," I replied. "I just remembered that I invited Clara Jean and her date to stop by for eggnog after their Christmas Eve dinner plans and, to my surprise, she accepted."

"Bourbon Balls *and* eggnog?" Blanche cocked her eyebrow at me disapprovingly.

"I'll get the non-alcoholic eggnog, if that'll make you feel better," I said.

The thought flashed through my mind that Blanche must have some newfound system of ethics because we had always had alcohol in the house, despite our Baptist affiliation. Walter was by no means a drunkard, but he did like to have his one glass of Scotch and water when he got home. I had personally never cared much for liquor, but we kept several bottles in our cabinet for the rare entertaining we did.

Blanche glared at me and I must have looked puzzled because she cut her eyes pointedly in Eddie's direction. He was picking slowly at his food and did not look up. I got the distinct feeling that he was well aware of the current exchange and wished he were anywhere else but there at the moment.

I may be a little slow, but I'm no idiot.

"You's all outta whiskey, Miz Ora. 'Member you had me pour all that out when Mr. Walter passed. Said it reminded you too much o' him to keep it around."

Well, I said no such thing, but I went along with the charade.

"That's right, I'd forgotten all about that. Well, there's no sense buying a whole new bottle of Jack Daniels for just a few little bourbon balls. I'll come up with something else to impress Clara Jean and her new beau."

I tried to sound nonchalant, but my response was stilted at best.

Later that night, after Blanche and the girls went home and Eddie turned in, I checked the liquor cabinet. It was empty, as I suspected. I didn't have time to ask Blanche about it at supper, but I assumed she had indeed poured out what little had been there. I'm not sure why I didn't know Eddie was an alcoholic. I suppose I should have wondered why a hardworking man was homeless, but instead I'd taken it for granted that he wanted it that way. It was years before I understood what Eddie would do for a roof over his head and three meals a day, and how much he would sacrifice for the daughter he loved.

I couldn't for the life of me figure out how Blanche knew to pour out the liquor, so I asked her the next day before Eddie got up.

"Some things you just know," was all she would allow.

We sat down later to make a list for our cookie baking adventure. I got out the recipes and Blanche calculated what we would need.

"Baking powder?" I read from the book.

"Pro'bly want to add that. What we got is pretty old," Blanche said.

"Vanilla extract ... should have plenty of that," I said and tried to skip over it.

"We out of vanilla, Miz Ora."

"We can't be out, Blanche. I just bought a huge bottle."

"We still out of it," she grumbled.

"Humor me and check, would you?" I was annoyed.

"I can check all day long, Miz Ora, and we'll still be outta vanilla."

She went to the pantry and brought back the eight ounce bottle I had recently purchased. She held it up to the light to prove that the bottle was indeed almost empty.

"What in the world happened?"

Blanche gave me the look that I'd become accustomed to getting from her. I don't think she meant to, but she had a way of making me feel like a pitiful old fool.

"Some things you just *know*," she repeated.

I added vanilla extract to the list.

Eddie tried his best to stay out of the way as preparation for the holidays proceeded, but Grace would have none of that. She was determined to have all the members of our improbable family together as much as possible. We grew accustomed to seeing Grace clutch Eddie's hand in both of hers and drag him down the hall toward whatever event or task we had going on at the time.

I thought that Eddie would eventually relax and allow himself to enjoy the attention, but he seemed to grow sadder by the minute. I made up my mind to ask him about it after the holidays passed and the excitement died down but, as usual, Gracie beat me to the punch.

We were up to our elbows in flour and sugar, our cookie baking expedition in full swing. I was rolling out cookie dough, ReNetta was cutting the shapes, Danita and Gracie were decorating and Blanche was baking the cookies and washing up dishes between batches. Eddie's job was to hold the old shoebox full of cookie cutters and dole them out at the appropriate time. We had stars of all sizes, bells and wreaths, snowmen, snowflakes, Christmas trees, reindeer and sleighs.

The girls were having great fun deciding how to decorate the cookies for maximum effect. When Eddie pulled out the Santa face cookie cutter and the girls cut the shape, Gracie was quick to point out a serious design flaw in our cookie project. Once the white sugar crystals went on for the beard and the red crystals adorned his hat, Santa was left with a decidedly pale complexion.

"Mama, how come we makin' Santy Claus's face so white?"

I'm not sure who was more horrified, me or Blanche. I thought back to the painting of the Last Supper above Blanche's red couch. It's funny what you take for granted when your view of the world reflects your own skin color.

Before Blanche could say a word, I roared, "Blanche! Get the cocoa!"

Well, that sent us all into fits of laughter that had Blanche and me crossing our legs and clutching our chests. I had never heard Eddie laugh before and I have to tell you, it was a magical sound. We laughed until our sides hurt, quieted down briefly and then started right back up again as soon as one of us replayed the scene in our heads. The little girls were only mildly amused and rolled their eyes in disgust when it took too long to collect ourselves.

We did pull out the cocoa, though. I blended it into one batch of buttery dough and let the girls cut it all into Santa faces. I have to admit, I liked the end result and I found myself wishing I'd thought to do it years earlier, when my cookies were being delivered to the families in Blanche's neighborhood.

We were putting the last batch into the oven when Grace noticed that Eddie had gone quiet again.

"Aw, Mr. Pecan," Grace crooned softly. She climbed gently into his lap and, resting her head back onto his shoulder, said, "Why you always so sad?"

He hugged her then. Tucked her head up under his chin and wrapped his arms around her little body.

"I'm sad 'cause I'm go'n miss you when I'm gone," he said.

"Where you going?" Gracie asked.

"I don't rightly know for sure, but I can't stay here forever."

"Why not?" Gracie wondered.

"'Cause this here ain't my home."

"Where is your home, then?"

Blanche interrupted then. "Gracie!"

"S'awright. She ain't botherin' me," Eddie said to Blanche. "I ain't got a home right now, child. I done left my home a long time ago."

"Can't you go back?" she asked.

"Too late to go back now," he said.

Nineteen

Christmas Eve dawned cold and crisp and the girls could barely contain themselves. Blanche and her family had been staying over every night since the weather turned too cold to walk home. Blanche and I opened the fourth bedroom upstairs, which had previously been used only for storage and was inclined to be a little cold in the winter and hot in the summer. I worried about putting the little girls in there until I remembered that Blanche's little house had no air-conditioning at all and only the one gas stove in the living room for heat. With one double bed and a pullout couch that had been bound for the Goodwill store just before Walter's death, there was plenty of room for the three younger girls to sleep and they were thrilled with the extra space. Blanche and Patrice took the pink room.

Out of all the events I had coordinated over the years, arranging a visit from Santa was nearly my undoing. I couldn't imagine how parents around the world handled the delivery schedules with a houseful of children underfoot. I had to make an excuse to send Eddie out to the garage when the bikes were delivered, while I entertained the girls inside. It took a bit of convincing to keep Grace from tagging along with him. She had become his shadow and was not inclined to let him out of her sight. I had a few last minute gifts to wrap and I enticed Grace to stay with me by sacrificing my usual gift-wrapping standards and allowing her to wrap them "all by herself."

The twins were excited to use the good china and silverware again and busied themselves with the now familiar process of setting the table. Blanche, thank goodness, had the dinner and dessert preparations under control or I'd have had a heap of trouble getting everything done.

It was decided that the girls would be allowed to open one gift that night, just after dinner. We had finished dessert and were just about to retire to the living room when Clara Jean and her date arrived. I was stunned to see Chip Smallwood without his uniform on. He looked as handsome as ever and I wondered why I had never thought of the two of them as a match.

Eddie looked a bit nervous when Chip entered, but he soon relaxed as we all sat by the fire sipping non-alcoholic eggnog and enjoying the excited chatter of the children opening their presents.

We sent the girls, even Patrice, to bed soon afterward. I pulled Chip aside and asked if he would help us get the bicycles from the garage once the girls were asleep.

It was no easy task getting those bicycles into the living room without waking everyone in the house. Even though I had them delivered fully assembled, it was after eleven o'clock when we finally got everything arranged just right.

I barely remember walking Chip and Clara Jean to the car.

"I'm so glad you could join us tonight," I said as Clara Jean leaned over and hugged me. "I hope it didn't take too much time away from your families."

"We enjoyed it, Miz Beckworth," Chip said. "I don't ever remember such a peaceful Christmas Eve."

Chip opened the passenger door, holding it long enough for Clara to slide gracefully into the low bucket seat. She winked at me as Chip went around the back of the car and opened the driver-side door.

"You approve?" she whispered.

"Very much so," I said.

"Merry Christmas to you both," I added as Chip slid behind the wheel and leaned over to smile at me.

"Merry Christmas!" they said at once.

Already synchronized, I thought as they pulled away. *That's a good sign.*

I have never heard such a racket as I did the next morning. The squeals of joy and excited laughter shook me from my sleep and I rushed to put my clothes on so I could join the family downstairs. Gracie met me at the top of the stairs.

"Miz Ora! Mr. Pecan," she called. "Come look at what Santy Claus brought us!"

I thought she would pull me off my feet going down those stairs.

Most of the gift-giving I'd done in the past had been accomplished anonymously or at least at arm's length. This was the first time I'd really experienced the joy firsthand. Gracie was beside herself with glee.

"It's got a *real horn,*" Gracie squealed as she squeezed the bulb attached to the handlebars of her new pink bike.

"Oh, Gracie," I exclaimed. "You must have been a really good girl this year."

"I was, Miz Ora. Really, *really* good."

ReNetta and Danita were equally thrilled. Danita pounced on the purple bike, proclaiming purple her "favoritest" color ever. ReNetta was happy with the orange one, since orange and black were her school colors.

"Oh!" she gasped as the thought came to her. "I can ride it in the spirit parade next year!"

"You better keep that thing nice, if you plannin' on doing that," Blanche spoke up.

"I'll wash it every day!"

I laughed. "I wouldn't go that far, honey."

After the other odds and ends were unwrapped, Eddie took the girls outside to try out the new bikes. Patrice stayed in to help clean up the living room.

Patrice was quiet as she picked up the crumpled wrapping paper and bows and stuffed them into a garbage bag. She liked her bicycle and the clothes I'd gotten at Penney's, I was sure of that, but she seemed distant and sad. I asked her about it after Blanche went to start breakfast for us.

"I'm all right, Miz Ora. Really."

"Something's bothering you, though. Is it Marcus?"

She nodded and her lips began to tremble as she fought for composure. She sat on the edge of the ottoman, resting her forearms on her legs.

"It's the first Christmas we've ever had like this."

"Without him, you mean?"

"Yeah. He was so excited about the Army, about having a real job and money to spend. He wanted to help Mama." Her voice broke and I waited, unable to speak.

"He wanted Christmas to be big this year. He was going to..."

My heart ached for her.

"He was going to get bicycles for the girls," she barely got the words out before breaking into sobs.

"Aw, honey," I said, moving to kneel before her, my hands on her knees. "I'm so sorry."

"It's okay, Miz Ora. You didn't know about the bikes. You didn't mean any harm."

I stood then, leaning over to catch Patrice's face in both hands. I pulled myself toward her and planted a kiss on the top of her head.

When I looked up, Blanche was standing at the edge of the dining room, wiping her hands on a kitchen towel and watching us intently. Without a word, she turned and went back into the kitchen.

The gaiety of the house returned when the girls came in to eat breakfast. Eddie's eyes were shining and the creases in his face seem amplified somehow. He kept his mouth closed as usual, but the rest of his face wore a happy grin.

Patrice remained quiet and so did Blanche. I found it very hard to make small talk, so I stayed quiet and listened to the chirping of the little birds at my table.

Twenty

Blanche never said another word about Eddie being there. Her children continued to come to the house each day and soon Grace had Eddie sipping fake tea from the tea set she found in the attic. Blanche and I eventually stopped holding our breaths every time Grace and Eddie interacted, but we still gasped aloud the night Grace brought up her "dream" at the dinner table.

Harley Odell had stopped by just as we were finishing dinner and I invited him to stay for coffee and dessert, which he accepted so eagerly I thought he must have timed the visit deliberately. Blanche had stood up to clear the table and fetch dessert and I was pouring coffee into the judge's cup when Grace piped up from out of the blue.

"I don't like bad dreams," she said.

Blanche dropped the plate she was holding. I startled so badly that I slung coffee across the tablecloth. There was no way to cover our reaction. Eddie cleared his throat. Harley leaned back in his chair and peered at me over the top of his glasses. I couldn't think of anything to say, so I said nothing. Blanche hastily made her retreat to the kitchen.

"Well," boomed the honorable judge, directing his attention to the child. "I don't like bad dreams either. Have you been having bad dreams, young lady?"

I held my breath and prayed. Eddie excused himself.

"Just one," Gracie said quietly. "But, I've had it a lotta times."

"I'm sorry to hear that," said the judge, leaning toward the child and lowering his voice soothingly. "You wanna tell me about it? Sometimes talking about it helps."

"No!" I said, more vehemently than I intended.

Harley tilted his head and frowned at me.

"What is the matter with you?"

I dabbed futilely at the still expanding coffee stain with my cloth napkin.

"It's not good for her to keep bringing up that dream. It isn't a pleasant one and it's certainly not appropriate for the dinner table." I felt like the proverbial deer in headlights. I was about to be run down and all I could do was watch it happen.

"Oh, come now," said Harley, genuinely confused. "How bad a dream can a child her age have?"

Blanche reappeared with peach cobbler and vanilla ice cream. Normally, she'd serve her own children last, but she put the biggest portion in front of Grace and said, "Eat up, now, chile'. That dream ain't go'n do you no harm and it can't come to no good talkin' about it all the time."

I think that was the moment that I really understood how long my own lie would live and how messy it could become. Neither Blanche nor I wanted the details of Gracie's "dream" to come to light, but for two vastly different reasons and only one similar one. I would never be free of it. And I wasn't sure I was smart enough to keep such an intricate lie straight.

"Well, I don't see the harm of letting the child talk about it—"

"Leave it alone, Harley," I said, this time intentionally firm. "It's not good table-talk."

Years on the bench gave Harley Odell an intuition as big as his beltline.

"What's your dream about, honey?"

"It's 'bout that white boy," Grace said matter-of-factly.

"Grace!" Blanche shushed her child. "Don't say 'white boy'—"

She stopped, horrified.

"I ain't talkin' 'bout his skin, Mama. I'm talkin' 'bout his hair. Whitest hair I ever saw."

"Gracie," I willed myself to be calm. "Why don't you take Mr. Eddie some cobbler and ice cream?"

"Okay," she said, and hopped down from her chair and took the bowl I held out to her.

"And when you're done, go on up and get your things. You got school tomorrow," Blanche added before retreating to the kitchen herself.

The moment Grace disappeared down the hall, Harley pushed back from the table and turned to face me.

"Is there something you're not telling me, Ora Lee?"

"About what, Harley?"

"Look, I don't know what's going on here, but I've had my suspicions for a while now. You and Blanche are acting a little strange, for lack of a better word. You're both jumpy as hell, not to mention that you obviously don't want me to know about that child's dream."

I sighed and pushed away from the table.

"Don't make a mountain out of a molehill, Harley," I said. "The child has had a rather graphic dream, which I have no doubt is caused by all the talk about that boy's death. We've heard it before and we've talked to her a great deal about it, but it is *not* a discussion I'd like to have at my dinner table and that's all there is to it. Now, finish your dessert and you can help me wash the dishes so Blanche can get on home."

Blanche's peach cobbler has a way of making a body forget anything else but the sheer pleasure of eating it. The rest of the evening went smoothly and Harley and I had a pleasant conversation over a second cup of coffee before he took his leave.

Twenty-one

The New Year brought new revelations about Eddie, some impressive, some heartbreaking. For one thing, I learned that Eddie received a pension of some sort, though he never said exactly what it was. It was delivered to the post office general delivery and Eddie rode Patrice's new bicycle to pick it up. I imagine that's how he went undetected. Most people recognized him immediately on the wrinkled old bike he rode before his arrest.

I didn't even know he was gone until he didn't show up for lunch. It wasn't unusual for him to sleep quite late, though sometimes he was up early puttering around the back yard or the garage. At any rate, when Blanche put sandwiches out for just the two of us, I finally got around to wondering about him.

"He's been gone all mornin'," Blanche said.

"All morning? What time did he leave?"

"He was headed off on Patrice's bike when I got here this mornin'. Said he was goin' to the post office to pick something up and he'd be back for lunch."

You can't imagine the thoughts that went through my head as concern for him settled in. First I worried that he'd been arrested again. He was not supposed to leave my house without telling me where he was going. It was part of the agreement for posting his bail.

Then I worried that he'd been killed. I was certain Ralph Kornegay would be happy to finish what he started. Then it occurred to me that I would lose fifty thousand dollars if Eddie disappeared and couldn't be found. I fretted myself into a frazzle by mid-afternoon.

When the girls came in from school, I told Blanche to take them on home. I needed help, but pickings were slim in the help department. Lord knows I couldn't call the police.

I picked up the phone to call Poopsie's office and thought better of it. But, thinking of the judge made me think of Clara Jean, and thinking of her put me in mind of Chip Smallwood. I called him at home and, mercifully, caught him on his day off. He was at my house fifteen minutes later and we formulated a plan together.

I could think of only two places Eddie might go. The first was to the Greyhound Bus Station down on Miller Street. I thought maybe he picked up money or even a ticket at the post office.

Clara Jean was much more graceful getting into Chip's car than I was. Even with Chip offering a steadying hand, I all but fell into the low bucket seat of the Camaro he drove. We headed to the bus station first, but the clerk there said no one had booked a ride at all that day.

"Do you think we could find out what he picked up at the post office?" I asked Chip.

"I really doubt it," he replied. "They aren't allowed to give out personal information like that."

The second place I thought of was a bar and I shared that with Chip.

"It's possible," he agreed. "That yellow bike shouldn't be too hard to spot if you want to just drive around and look."

"The Shamrock isn't too far from the post office," I said, offering up one of the only bar and liquor stores that came to mind.

Chip chuckled. "I doubt he'd go there, Ma'am. He'd most likely head for one where he wouldn't stick out like a sore thumb."

"Oh, right," I said, feeling silly again.

"I know of a few we might check, though. The County Line Bar is just south of town. He might be behind the line."

"Behind the line?" I wondered.

"It's a window at the back of the bar. That's where blacks are served."

I think I gasped aloud because Chip went on quickly.

"Yeah, it bothers me, too. There's no real rule about it, so it's hard to fix the problem."

"I had no idea," I murmured, more to myself than to Chip.

"Fact is, blacks could go inside and the bartender would serve them, but it wouldn't take long for the patrons to make them feel plenty unwelcome."

I was too stunned to speak. I sat numbly as Chip headed south of town and cruised through the parking lot of the County Line Bar. We drove past a few old pickup trucks, one rumpled sedan and a work van with a logo and contact information crudely painted on the side. *Chuck's*

Handyman Servis You name it, we fix it. Resonable rates.

As we rounded the building, I caught sight of a small clearing in the woods just behind the parking lot. A rusted barrel puffed dark smoke into the air. It was surrounded by a circle of cast off chairs and squatty stumps of once large trees. Only one old man sat nearby and he was far too big to be Eddie. I glanced at the back of the building and noticed the window Chip spoke of, but there was no yellow bike parked in the area at all.

"It's weird, isn't it?" Chip offered. "Who would think this was still going on?"

"Do you see a lot of this at work?"

"Every day," Chip nodded and pulled out of the parking lot back toward town.

We went down Pine Street, the main drag through colored town. I had never, in all my years, been down that street. The houses were colorful and small. Dogs and chickens wandered freely in front yards and under porches. A small general store I didn't know existed bore a battered screen door with a Sunbeam Bread logo rusting across its middle.

Nearing the end of the street, people were lined up at the open window of a small, faded green block building. The smell of hickory smoke was enticing and I could see that it came from behind the place.

"Cal's Ribs," Chip said. "Best you'll ever eat. He's only open three days a week and there's always a line."

"Smells wonderful," I offered, though I couldn't imagine myself eating ribs of any kind. Too messy, I thought.

Chip pointed out another bar, though you'd not have known it from the street. There were no signs to indicate that it was anything other than an abandoned storefront. There was still no yellow bike in sight.

"Anywhere else you can think of?" Chip asked.

I started to shake my head no, but a thought leaped to mind as if it had been sitting there waiting all along.

"The woods," I said, nodding triumphantly.

Chip smiled. "Yep, the woods."

We found Eddie easily. Chip knew the spot well, he told me later. There was a low fire burning among a circle of small rocks. The first thing I thought when I saw him was, *He's sitting on a throne.*

On second glance, I realized it was an ancient barber's chair, the bottom section made of ornate metal and the cushions covered with red leather that had seen much better days. I would find out later that it was stuffed with horse hair, but at first it just looked like an odd piece of furniture to find in the middle of the woods.

A paper bag sat on the metal stand to which the chair was mounted. Eddie was quite still as we approached, his chin resting on his chest. Then his head snapped upright suddenly and he reached down and grasped the paper bag without looking.

"Eddie?" I spoke softly. "What are you doing here?"

His head jerked again and he looked in our direction, straining, it seemed, to bring us into focus.

"Aw, hey, Miz Ora," Eddie tried to enunciate carefully, but it only served to slur his words even more. "Who dat you got with you?"

"It's me, Mr. Mims." Chip spoke softly. "Chip Smallwood."

Eddie squinted again.

"You comin' to take me back to jail?" he asked.

"No, Eddie, not to jail. I came to take you home."

"Ain't got no home." Eddie wobbled a bit, but reached down and brought the bag to his mouth for a drink.

"Sure you do, Eddie," I said. "Your home's with us right now."

"Naw, it ain't. Used to have a home in Alabama. I ever tell you 'bout Alabama?"

"No," I said. "You never have."

"Had me a girl in 'bama. Tressa. Tressa Lee Mims. Pretty girl, too. Her mama took good care of her. Grow'd her up good and fine."

"Tressa," I repeated. "Pretty name. She's your daughter?"

"Yup, my baby girl. Had another one, too, but I lost her a long time ago."

Chip and I exchanged looks. Neither of us was sure what to do, so we stood there for a few minutes.

"You ready to go home, Eddie?" I was the first to break the silence.

"Can I take my chair?" he asked, as if it were the most reasonable question in the world.

"Um," I started, but Chip cut me off.

"I'll come back and get it for you tomorrow, Eddie. I can't fit it in my car today."

"You'll get it tomorrow?"

"Tomorrow. I promise."

"Can I bring my bottle?"

Oh, Lord, I thought. *Give me the right words now.*

"Let's leave it here, Eddie. If you still want it tomorrow, Chip can bring it when he gets your chair. That sound okay?"

"Yeah, okay," he said and tipped the bottle to his mouth again.

Chip took the bag from his hand and set it on the ground.

"Come on, buddy, let's get you home," he said and helped Eddie from the chair.

Eddie cooperated, trying to stand on his own, but taking the help that was offered. Then he stopped suddenly and leaned away from Chip to look at his face.

"I didn't kill that boy," Eddie said.

Lord, Jesus, help me. I froze for a moment, purely unable to move or speak.

"Miz Ora, tell him. Tell him I didn't kill that boy."

"Eddie, he knows you didn't kill anybody." My voice was rattling like coins in a tin can.

"He knows?"

"He knows you didn't kill anyone," I repeated.

Chip looked at me then and the question was there on his face. I could see it, plain as day.

"Tha's good," Eddie mumbled and sighed hard. "Let's go home now."

There are so many things about this time in my life that I swear I could never imagine happening to me. This was a scene out of the Twilight Zone. Chip Smallwood, half-carrying a drunk old man to his car, with me toddling along behind pushing a bright yellow bicycle, in shoes that were never meant for walking in the woods. Standing at the car, a two door coupe, I tried to figure out which of the only two options would be the least difficult to accomplish. Either I had to crawl into the back seat, dress and all, or Chip would have stuff the barely conscious Eddie in there somehow. I swallowed my dignity and folded myself behind the bucket seat on the passenger side. Getting out would be the real test, I learned shortly thereafter.

Chip managed to fit Patrice's bike in his trunk with the front wheel and handlebars hanging out over the bumper. He tied the trunk lid down with a shoelace.

Eddie was asleep before we'd traveled the few blocks to my house. Chip carried him from the car, just picked him up like a child and deposited him into his bed. I made a pot of coffee as Chip got Eddie undressed and covered him up.

I was pouring two cups when Chip appeared in the dining room. He took the coffee gratefully.

"Do you need me to stay tonight?" he asked.

"No, I don't think so."

"He's probably out for the night anyway."

"Most likely," I agreed.

"This isn't good." Chip said.

"Nope. Not good at all."

"I have to report it, you know."

"I figured as much."

We sat silently for a few minutes. The question still hung there, but it was never spoken aloud, nor answered. Harley Odell was on my porch the very next day.

The meeting went well, I thought. Harley explained to Eddie that he would revoke his bail if Eddie drank again. Eddie quietly acknowledged that he understood.

Harley asked where he got the alcohol and Eddie told how he cashed his meager monthly check and used part of it to buy liquor.

"Where's the rest?" Harley asked.

"I got a little savings account my daughter Tressa keeps for me. I get me a money order from the bank and send it down there. Sometimes I keep enough for food, but I most times spend it on the bottle if I keep it long enough."

"Ever thought about getting help, Mr. Mims?"

"Thought about it. Reckon I could go to the VA if I had a mind to, but I don't rightly care for doctors in the first place. And the military ain't exactly been the best move I ever made, neither."

"You serve in the war?" Harley asked.

"Sho' nuff did."

"Where'd you train?"

"Alabama mostly."

"Tuskegee?" Harley asked hesitantly.

"Mmm-hmmm," Eddie nodded.

"Jesus H. Christ," Harley whispered and the meeting was over.

Twenty-two

Just after Harley Odell left my house, Eddie went to his room "for a rest" he said. He came back out fifteen minutes later and announced that he had made a decision he thought I ought to hear. We walked into the back yard for privacy.

"I'd like to talk to my lawyer today, if I can," he began.

"I think I can arrange that," I said. "Is there any specific reason why?"

"I'm going to change my plea to guilty, Miz Ora," he said, as if it were the most rational thing he'd ever done.

"Eddie, I can't let you do that." I sounded more tired than emphatic, so I repeated myself. "I just can't let you do it."

"With all due respect, Miz Ora, you can't really stop me. It's the best thing to do and I know it, sho' as I'm sittin' here right now."

"Why do you say that?"

"'Cause it's true. I'm gettin' too old and tired and sick to live like I been livin'."

"But what's that got to do with going to jail?"

"It's the safest place for me. They got a bed and a toilet and three meals a day, and it won't cost me a dime."

It sounded so logical that I almost agreed on the spot. It might not seem possible, but my conscience was wreaking havoc on my heart. Even I had to admit his confession was just too convenient for me. I was willing to risk a trial and hope for acquittal, any small chance that I might not have to admit what I had done for Marcus. I swear though, by all that's holy, if a jury had found him guilty, I'd have owned up to it. I'd have come forward and taken my punishment, whatever it would be.

But I could not let him plead guilty.

"Eddie," I said, and my voice broke. I reached over and laid my hand on his painfully thin knee. "Eddie," I tried again.

"I done made up my mind, Miz Ora, and I really don't want you to change it for me."

"I can't do it, Eddie. You'll die in there."

"Better'n dyin' in the woods, ain't it?"

"I don't know how to answer that question. I just know I can't let you pay a debt you don't owe."

"I reckon I'm the bes' judge of that. Sometimes the debt you pay ain't exactly the one you owe, but it works out jus' the same anyway. Lord knows I done caused my share of heartache in this life."

"Haven't we all?"

"Miz Ora, I jus' want you to sit there and think about it hard now. Let's say you did tell the truth 'bout what you know. What good that go'n do?"

I pulled my cardigan tight around my shoulders and stared at the empty garage in front of me.

"The truth won't bring neither of those boys back to they mama's. Won't bring Grace no comfort. Won't do nothin' for Blanche but cause her more heartache. You know this town won't believe nothin' they hear. They'll believe exactly what they want to. Whites'll take one side and blacks'll take the other, and never the twain shall meet."

I tried to swallow the lump in my throat, but my neck burned with the effort and tears spilled down my face.

"This is just such a mess. How did I make such a mess, Eddie?"

"I don't reckon it was your doin', Miz Ora. You did what you thought was best. Things was just against us all along. But, now that you mention it, you could be in a heap of trouble for not saying nothin' about Marcus."

"You let me worry about that. I won't have you taking the rap for me, Eddie."

"Ain't tryin' to. I'm jus' tryin' to do the right thing."

"Don't do anything yet. Let me think about it awhile, could you?"

"There's just one more thing I gotta say 'bout this."

I looked up at him and he swallowed hard and continued, "I been tryin' half my life to stop drinkin', but I come to think it just ain't no use. I don't want to go to my grave bein' a slave to the bottle. I just want to talk to Mr. Thatcher and see can he make me a bargain or somethin'."

"A plea bargain?"

"Yeah, that's it. I don't wanna fry in no 'lectric chair. I jus' wanna live in peace, that's all. Think they'll let me do that?"

I couldn't answer. I turned to go back into the house and, as I lifted my head to look where I was going, I thought I saw a flash of white going from the back porch into the kitchen. I left Eddie sitting in the back yard and went to my room, and I didn't come out until time for supper.

The next day, I called Jeffery Thatcher and asked him to meet with Eddie at my house. We settled on a time that afternoon and I concentrated on getting the house ready to receive a guest. Eddie put on a nice suit from Walter's closet. It hung a little loose and the shoes were a size too large, but Eddie shined them up with the little shoeshine kit from Walter's room. He looked downright handsome, if a little stiff, sitting on the edge of my couch.

Mr. Thatcher arrived on time and I left them alone to work out whatever deal they could. I knew, sure as I was living and breathing, that I would say something to mess things up or give my secret away.

I took a walk to calm my nerves. I passed J.C. Penney's and Ezell's Department store. I stopped at the window of Geiger's Dress Shop and watched Gladys Humphrey pick out a new dress for her daughter's upcoming wedding. I poked my head in at Dick Thomas's jewelry store and said hello to Dick and Ellie and their sales clerk, Patty. I went into the Woolworth store and ordered a cherry coke to go. When I finally made it home, Jeffrey's car was gone and Eddie and Blanche were sitting on the front porch, bundled against the chilly winter air.

"Well?" I asked.

"He says he go'n talk to the prosecutor and let me know tomorrow. I reckon he's worried about the Kornegay family puttin' up a fuss."

I nodded once and went inside. I'd sworn off my meddling that very morning and here it was, not even dinnertime, and I was picking up the phone again. I called Ralph Kornegay and arranged to meet him in the church parking lot the next day.

Twenty-three

Eddie's arraignment was scheduled for January 26th, 1977. That left him a little less than two weeks of freedom and I was bound and determined to make that time nice for him. Chip borrowed his father's pickup truck and went back to Eddie's camp in the woods to pick up his old chair. It was a beautiful thing, despite having been in the open for God knows how long. Eddie came outside to help decide where the chair would go and we chose a cozy spot where the yard made a little alcove beside the garage. He wanted to fix it up though, so we put it in the garage first, right in the empty spot where Walter's car once sat.

"Where in the world did you find this chair, Eddie?"

He chuckled when I asked him that.

"You ain't go'n believe this, Miz Ora, but I only paid ten dollars for that ol' thing."

"You're kidding."

It was hard to believe. The chair must have once sat in a fairly nice barber shop, judging by the ornate scrollwork in the metal base.

"Nope," he laughed "Ten dollars I paid and had it delivered to boot."

"Delivered?"

"Yes'm, out to the woods."

"Good Lord," I said, "How in the world did you manage that?"

"Used to hop me a freight train every now and again, jus' to get away for awhile. Sometimes I'd go all the way to Alabama to see Tressa. Most times I'd just go down the tracks and back. Used to see this here chair, jus' sittin' in the back yard of this man's house. Wasn't all that far from here, just out by the Minute Maid plant."

Not far from Blanche's house, I thought to myself.

"Then one day, when I got my check cashed and had some money to spend, I hopped off the freight car—they always switchin' cars out there, so it goes real slow—and I asked that ol' man 'bout this chair."

Eddie went on to tell how the man said for five dollars he could take it right then. Eddie couldn't figure out how to get it back to the woods, so he offered the man ten dollars if he would get his nephew to deliver it. They made the deal right then and Eddie paid him when they got to the woods with the chair.

Eddie spent the next week fixing the chair up with tools he found in the garage. I found some old red vinyl in my fabric stash, left over from recovering some dinette chairs we had in the fifties, and we recovered the seat and back of the barber's chair with it. That's when we discovered the seat had been stuffed with horse hair, which I knew indicated quality in the manufacturing.

When it was done, Eddie decided he rather liked the chair in the garage and, since there wasn't likely to be another car in that spot anytime soon, I agreed to leave it where it was. Eddie spent as much time as possible out there before his court date. If he drank at all, I didn't see or smell the alcohol.

Eddie was clean and sober the day of his arraignment and he went to court in the same suit he wore to talk to his lawyer the weeks before.

The Kornegay family was not in the courtroom. I'm not sure what Ralph said to the rest of his family to keep them away, but he managed it well. There were only a few local reporters and a handful of townsfolk there to witness Eldred Mims plead guilty to the charge of Second Degree Murder. In a deal with the county prosecutor and the Honorable Judge Harley T. Odell, Eddie was sentenced immediately to twenty-five years to life, whichever came first.

Blanche and I sat in the second row, directly behind Eddie. I sat with a straight back, one gloved hand clutching Blanche's bare one. She held a handkerchief in her other hand and dabbed at her eyes throughout the proceeding, but didn't make a sound until they placed the cuffs on his wrists and led him away.

Then she groaned softly and began to mumble, "This ain't right, Miz Ora. This ain't right."

"Blanche," I whispered. "Shhh, now...shhh."

She quieted down, but continued to cry. The bailiff adjourned the court, Poopsie retired to his quarters and we sat until everyone else had left. We were just standing to leave when the good judge appeared in his doorway and motioned us into his office. I shook my head in protest and he came to us instead.

"You okay?" he asked.

"I've been better."

"Anything you want to tell me now? Last chance, Ora. After today, I really don't want to know."

"I believe it's all been said now, Harley."

"Same for you, Blanche?"

She stood and looked him square in the eye and I thought it was all over for us. But she turned without a word and left the courtroom. Harley sighed and gave me a hard, perplexed look. I returned his gaze until I had to look away.

"Good day, Mrs. Beckworth," he said and returned to his office without so much as a backward glance.

It *had* all been said, as far as I was concerned. Ralph Kornegay knew the truth—the whole ugly truth—and I left it up to him to decide which way the ball would bounce. If he interfered or caused Eddie any further harm, I would tell everything, and I meant everything, including what Skipper did to Grace and what I did to cover up for Marcus. Prison be damned, the town would know the truth.

It hurt to watch the man receive my news. He may have been ignorant; he may even have been a bigot, but he was a father first and his pain was raw. I remember thinking it was odd that Ralph never once tried to deny what Skipper had done. He was silent at first; then he asked one pointed question after another until he had no more to ask.

I gave him the names of the boys who I believed were with him that day. His shoulders dropped with each name I spoke until I thought he would disappear beneath the seat of his patrol car. He never condemned or threatened me. He simply received the news, asked his questions, nodded his acceptance of my terms and drove away. We never spoke again after the day I delivered my ultimatum. Not once. Ralph was dead of a heart attack within a year. His wife survived him by only two years. If he ever told her about their son, I never knew and never wanted to know.

Twenty-four

Eddie was sent to the state corrections facility just outside of town. They took him that very day. Blanche and I returned home from the courthouse in complete silence; neither of us daring to speak a word. I directed the cab to Blanche's house first, even though the day was barely half over.

She opened the car door, then asked without even a glance my way, "What about yo' supper?"

"I can manage," I said, my voice sharper than I intended.

"Girls'll be there off the bus."

"I'll call the school."

"What am I going to tell them about Eddie?"

I knew full well that was not a question that needed an answer, but I forged ahead anyway.

"Tell them Eddie loves them. More than they will ever know."

She got out of the cab then, and hauled herself up the sidewalk and into the house. I could feel her weight as if it were cast upon my own frame. I had not known sadness to feel heavy before, not even when Walter died. That grief was weightless, almost buoyant, as if I could feel myself floating toward some enormous abyss. It was not a good feeling, mind you. It was more like having been tethered by a lifeline and being cut loose in a gentle, but persistent tide.

This grief pressed down like gravity amplified. The seat of the cab cut into the backs of my legs and my head would not rest squarely on my shoulders, but bobbed uncomfortably between the headrest and my collar bones. I could barely gather myself out of the vehicle when the driver pulled up to my house. I gave him a twenty and did not wait for change.

The first time I visited Eddie in prison, I went alone. I wasn't sure who would be on his visitors' list, so I didn't risk having the children turned away. As it turned out, had I not brought a batch of Blanche's oatmeal cookies, I might not have been received myself. Seems Eddie decided not to allow visitors at all. Negotiations were brief. The cookies came in with me or went home the same way. Never underestimate the power of baked goods. I was sitting across a table from him within five minutes.

Eddie looked drawn that first visit, but it was only a week after his arraignment. By the time I made my fourth weekly trip, Eddie had already filled out a bit and his eyes had lost their yellowish glaze. Blanche and I visited when we could. We still took treats every now and then and made sure he had books and magazines to read. I waited each time for him to tell me he wanted out of there, but he never did. He seemed happy and healthy and he even gained a bit of weight, which he swore was from Blanche's cookies.

Our visits became less frequent as we focused on Patrice's graduation and all it entailed. We had already measured her for cap and gown when I thought to ask her where she had applied to go to college.

"College?" She seemed almost indignant. "I didn't apply to any college at all, Miz Ora."

"Well, why in the world not?" I asked.

"Because we can't afford college."

"Well, what about scholarships? You made good grades; you're in the National Honor Society, for crying out loud."

"I don't think that's enough to get me the kind of scholarship I'd need. Mama doesn't make much money and ... oh, sorry, Miz Ora, I didn't mean any disrespect. I just don't think we can afford it, that's all."

I don't know why I just assumed Patrice was preparing for college. When I was in school, I spent the better part of my junior and senior years researching, visiting and applying to schools I thought I might want to attend.

"Patrice Lowery! You mean to tell me you wrote off college that quickly, with no attempt whatsoever? Don't you want to go to college?"

"Well, yeah, of course I do. I just don't really know how to go about it, I guess."

"What did your guidance counselor say about applying?" I asked.

"She never said anything. She helped me choose courses at the beginning of each year, but we never talked about college."

I could feel the fury rise up in my throat. I wondered how many other promising students were falling through gaping holes in the school system. I wanted to lash out at someone and I almost picked up the phone that very minute. But then it occurred to me that I had done nothing to help her either. Besides, I knew what my meddling had done in the past. I was determined to be more deliberate in any future acts.

"Patrice...honey. Promise me one thing, would you?"

"I'll try," she answered wisely.

"Promise me that, from now on, if you ever want to do anything in your life—anything at all—you'll ask someone for help if you need it."

"Okay," she said vaguely, as if she thought I was a little off my rocker.

"What were you planning on doing after high school?"

"I was just going to work, I guess. Mama needs help with the girls and I want to buy a car. They said I could go full-time at the grocery store whenever I wanted."

"Okay, that's what you planned. Now, what do you *want*? If you could make your dreams come true just by dreaming them, what would you do?"

Patrice looked down then, as if she were embarrassed by her own thoughts.

"Promise you won't laugh?"

"Cross my heart and hope to die."

"I always wanted to be a lawyer."

Sweet Jesus, here we go again.

Twenty-five

Walter Beckworth was a planner. His attention to detail and thrift were unrivaled in my book. When he died, I had little to do except open the file marked *Funeral Arrangements* and follow his instructions. Our caskets, plots and headstones were already purchased, the funeral home pre-paid. There was a page marked "Songs for Memorial Service" with separate columns for Walter and me. We never actually discussed these plans, but under my name he included all my favorite hymns, as if I had chosen them myself. "How Great Thou Art", "In the Garden", "My Jesus, As Thou Wilt" and "Abide With Me" were all listed there in Walter's precise and patient hand.

Of course, in his line of work, Walter was well-insured and I lacked for nothing before or after his death. I lived comfortably and easily continued to pay Blanche a decent salary for keeping my home. Truth be known, however, I had no need for a full-time housekeeper now that I was no longer involved in the day to day business of being Walter's wife.

Patrice's dream changed all that. When I exhausted all the avenues I could take to get financial aid for a bright young black woman who excelled in school, I found that the task was more difficult than I imagined.

And so it was that, at the arguably ancient age of 58, I went back to work. Walter's foresight allowed his insurance agency to continue to run long after his death. His plan was to give me time to sufficiently recover from the loss of my husband before I decided what to do. At that point, I could sell, dissolve or continue to run the company as I saw fit. Quite frankly, when his Last Will and Testament was read, I laughed out loud at that declaration. What did I know about running an insurance agency and what would possess Walter to include such an option? The only questions I have now are: how did he know? And how did I *not* know my own husband like he knew me?

Patrice applied and was accepted to the University of Florida's pre-law program. Aside from the small academic scholarship she was awarded, the money came straight from a scholarship fund I set up through the agency. The fund is still operating today and continues to help deserving young women achieve their goals. In all the charitable work I ever did, the food lines, the Christmas baskets, the donations made with smug satisfaction, this was the thing of which I was most proud.

Patrice knew only that I found a scholarship for her and she was beside herself with joy. So was I. Blanche, of course, worried about everything. Would Patrice have a place to live? How would she eat? Who would pay for clothing and other incidentals while she studied? I read the award citation out loud to her and filled in details as needed. In a way, Patrice was the test model for the future recipients of the scholarship. Anytime Blanche came up with a question, or financial issues arose, I amended the trust fund to accommodate the needs.

The tuition, room and board was covered in full and an additional stipend paid so that the recipient's job, for the duration of her academic years, was to earn her chosen degree.

For the next twenty years, which seems hard to believe given my age, I went to the office three days a week and paid myself an additional salary which went exclusively to the scholarship fund. I resumed my community involvement, as I had done when Walter was alive, though now my networking was aimed specifically at fundraising for the non-profit portion of the agency.

As soon as I started working again, I gave Blanche a raise, mostly for putting up with me. When she balked at being paid more than she deemed the job worth, I increased her workload. She never complained again.

Blanche began accompanying me to various charitable events, and I realized the uniform would have to go. I cringe now when I think of how long I kept my invaluable friend and helpmate in those crisp white symbols of servitude. I've always said that the worst thing anyone could ever say about me was, "She means well," but I have to claim now that I meant well. I meant for her uniforms to be part of her pay. I meant for it to be easy for her to wash them. I meant to help her avoid bleach spills and food stains on her own clothing. I never meant to put her in her place, but that's just what I did. And, God help me, it took Dovey Kincaid to make me realize it.

It was Thanksgiving of 1979 and Patrice was home from college for a few days. The younger girls were out of school and stayed home with their older sister while Blanche and I went to the church to help distribute food among the baskets to be delivered. We were working in the kitchen of the fellowship hall, which was fairly large, but a bit cramped with ten to twelve of us working side-by-side.

When Dovey dropped a jar of pickles, shattering the glass and spraying sugary green juice everywhere, she spoke without hesitation.

"Oh, dear, look what I've done! Blanche, could you grab the mop and clean that up for me, please?"

I froze immediately, which halted the entire distribution line. Blanche didn't react at all, except to head for the broom closet.

"Whoa, whoa, WHOA!" I said, as I found my voice. Blanche stopped abruptly. Dovey, who had marched right over to the sink and grabbed a wet towel to clean herself up, spun around with a bewildered expression on her face. All eyes were on me, all wondering what had just prompted my outburst. I didn't even try to disguise my contempt.

"You made the mess, Dovey. *You* clean it up."

I never meant to humiliate Blanche, though I think I did. There was no way to recover from it. No matter how you look at it, Blanche had just received two direct orders and neither of us considered what a horrible position they put her in.

"I don't mind helpin', Miz Ora," she said after a moment of awkward silence.

"Neither do I," I said as I dropped out of the assembly line and followed Blanche to the closet.

I could hear murmuring behind me as the women resumed their tasks, but I never worried or even wondered what they were talking about. *Good,* I thought. *Let them figure it out for themselves.* Dovey joined us in the clean up and we silently mopped and swept and wiped away the evidence of our mistake.

Blanche never wore a uniform again. When I asked her not to, she did not ask why. In her usual candid way, she said simply, "I can change my clothes, Miz Ora, but I can't change my color. They's always gonna be people who expect what they expect."

"You're absolutely right, Blanche," I nodded. "And I can't change anyone's expectations but my own."

Twenty-six

After Patrice went away to college, the girls rode the bus to my house every day after school. Neither Blanche nor I would even dream of having them stay home alone. Re'Netta and Danita excelled in school, just as their older sister had. Grace did not do as well. Blanche would often get notes home saying Grace had trouble staying focused and on task in the classroom. When she entered the third grade, she was assigned to a trim, pretty, blonde teacher named Miss Folsom. Grace liked her well enough at first, but she began to withdraw after the first few weeks of school.

Blanche asked her what was wrong, but Grace would only say things like, "Miss Folsom got mad at me today." Or "I don't think Miss Folsom likes me."

Blanche was obviously not happy, but she didn't say anything about it until Grace came home in tears with a note for "The Parents of Grace Lowery."

Miss Folsom was apparently at her wit's end, and I'm using the term "wit" rather loosely here, because Grace could not seem to finish her work in class. Her solution, according to the note, was to send Grace to the principal's office to be paddled for her offense.

"The very idea," I nearly shouted, "of paddling a child for not finishing the outlining of simple letters when she can already read a book, is absolutely asinine."

"She can't be disrupting the class, though," Blanche reasoned.

"Disrupting the class?" I exploded. "It doesn't say a word about disrupting the class. It says she's not finishing her work. It says she has been separated from the class by a dividing screen and moved away from the window so she won't be distracted or inclined to daydream. It doesn't say anywhere that she's bothering anyone at all. This is wrong,

Blanche. This is not Grace's fault."

I felt so protective of Grace, in that moment and for years afterward, that I literally trembled with anger.

"What do you think I should do, then?" Blanche asked.

"Well, for one thing, I think you should make it clear that Grace will certainly *not* be spanked for something she has no control over."

"But she's got to finish her work," Blanche said.

"I agree," I said, "but it won't help her a bit to be frightened into finishing it. For God's sake, Blanche, hasn't she been through enough?"

I regretted those words the moment they left my mouth. Blanche stiffened immediately and glared at me with as much disdain as I have ever seen aimed in my direction.

"You ain't got to tell me what she's been through, Miz Ora."

"Blanche, I'm sorry," I began.

"I know exactly what my child has been through," she continued. "And I know it ain't gonna get any easier for her, that's for sure. But she got to do the same as every other child in that classroom, and that includes finishing her work, no matter how boring it may be."

"Blanche, listen to me," I pleaded. "I know she has to do her work. I know she has to find her way in the world, but this teacher does not like her and you and I both know why."

"So, I'll ask you again. What do you think I should do?"

"I think you should have her moved to another classroom."

"Huh," Blanche grunted. "They ain't gonna move her on my account. I can tell you that right now."

"They'll move her on mine," I said, ignoring the second round of regret I felt.

"And you think that'll help her? You throwin' your weight around for my child?" She grunted again. "Shows what you know."

I sighed then and sat down at the table, putting my head in my hands. What *did* I know? I'd never had a child of my own and, Lord knows I'd never been colored. Didn't matter what the rules *should* be. It matters what they are, if you're going to play the game.

"I think we should get Gracie some help, Blanche." I said wearily. "And you know what I mean, so don't even act like you don't."

"I am helpin', Miz Ora," Blanche said. "I'm helpin' her live in this world."

"But she needs more..."

"I'll see can I get her changed to another teacher," Blanche interrupted, "but I don't wanna hear another word about help. I'm helpin' her the best I can, and that's gonna have to do."

"But if she can just *talk* to someone about it," I tried again.

"I done made up my mind, Miz Ora. What's done is done and we all just got to move on. You say another word about it and I'll quit."

My head snapped up then.

"I'm serious. I'll quit and go home. I got to put this behind me now. I can't be talkin' about it and thinkin' about it and cryin' over it every time I turn around. And I can't have you runnin' around tryin' to fix everything, either. We got to live in this world, Miz Ora, and we got to do it on our own."

I stood then and faced her, fighting back the tears I felt stinging my eyes.

"Blanche, I'm sorry about all this."

"I know," she said, softening. "But, Eddie was right. Things was just against us all along. We all did what we thought was right and now we just got to live with it."

And so our vow was made and sealed and never broken as long as Blanche was alive. We did not speak of it again.

Chip and Clara Jean married in the spring of 1979. Always the prudent one, Clara Jean insisted on a long engagement, though I'm certain Chip would have had her at the altar far sooner than she allowed. They eventually had two sons, who are the spitting image of their daddy. Chip quit the sheriff's department after a few years and transferred to the Mayville Correctional Facility, where Eddie lived the remainder of his life. I often wondered if he had done that as a favor to me. He had, after all, promised to look after Eddie for me, though I never expected him to take his responsibility to that level. Clara assures me it was nothing more than a financial decision and I hope that's true. She continued to work for Judge Odell until he retired in 1983 and then she stayed home with her sons. They have done well and I am as proud of them as if they belonged to me alone.

By the time Grace was eighteen years old in 1988, she had two children, not much more than a year apart. She dropped out of school when she got pregnant the first time. It was hard for me to watch her life unravel the way it did. I wanted to help her, but Blanche kept her away from me for the most part. I suppose she figured I had already done enough.

Grace stayed home with her children during the day, but I found out soon enough that Blanche kept them at night while Grace went out. That must have been when Grace started doing drugs.

The twins graduated in 1984. Sweet, quiet Danita married her high school sweetheart within the year. She grew up with Curtis Bledsoe and knew his heart was for the Lord. They moved away for a time, while Curtis went to Bible College and became a pastor, then they moved back to Mayville and started a family together. They are together to this day.

ReNetta went to a cosmetology school after she graduated. She has never married and is a hairdresser at a local salon. I always thought that was a perfect vocation for her, something that would always satisfy her inquisitive mind and creative spirit. She's good at it, too. She stops by every now and then with pictures of the hair shows she does. My goodness, I never knew how many wild and intricate styles were possible with hair. I've kept the same simple hairstyle I've worn for as many years as I have been gray. ReNetta has tried to get me to go for something different, but I put my foot down on that one.

Twenty-seven

1998 was a tough year for us. I was approaching my 80th birthday and slowing down fast. Blanche was a few years shy of her 60th and doing just fine. I don't know what I would have done without her. She was the reason I was able to work as long as I did. She basically handled everything; I was just along for the ride.

Blanche was also raising Grace's children by herself. Grace started out disappearing for days at a time. Blanche had Shawn and Rochelle start riding the bus to my house when she realized she just couldn't count on Grace being home in the afternoons. I was happy for them to be there. I'd learned long ago to enjoy a full house.

Eventually, Grace was gone for good, or at least for several years. She didn't leave a note, but word got out to Blanche that she'd run off with a known drug dealer and pimp. We both began to tire easily.

Once again, we dropped out of the various clubs and charitable organizations to which we now *both* belonged, and this time it was for good.

I knew I was not going to live forever and, even though Walter had made many plans of his own, I hadn't really done all the planning I should have in anticipation of my own mortality.

I had no heirs, no one to take over Walter's business or care about my personal effects. I sat for hours on end, rocking on the front porch, wondering what in the world I would do.

Patrice was an attorney by then and worked for a firm near the courthouse. They did mostly criminal law, and Patrice did quite a bit of pro bono work in the community on her own time. She stopped by my house fairly often. I knew she was really coming to see Blanche, but she spent time with me, too, and I enjoyed seeing and talking with her.

On one of her visits—it was early spring, I remember, because the flowers were blooming but it was still cool enough to enjoy the porch. Anyway, on one of her visits, Patrice brought up the subject of the Pecan Man.

"I saw Eddie last week, Miz Ora," Patrice said. "He said to tell you hello."

"Eddie," I said fondly. "How is he doing?"

"He's getting old and frail, but he says he's doing fine. I left him playing a rousing game of dominoes the other day. He keeps the young guys on their toes, I can tell you that."

"I think I always underestimated the man," I admitted.

Patrice laughed. "I don't think you were the only one who underestimated him. I've learned quite a bit about him lately."

"Do you go out to see him often?"

"Not as much as I would like, but I try to stop in when I have to make a trip to the prison, or when Mama bakes him some cookies. I'm the most popular attorney out there."

"I'll just bet you are," I laughed.

"I've been thinking of reopening Eddie's case." Patrice dropped that bombshell like it was just another batch of cookies and, Lord help me, it was as if someone had touched me with a cattle prod. My skin tingled with the shock for several minutes and I had trouble gathering my thoughts to respond. If Patrice noticed, she didn't let on.

"Something just bothers me about the whole thing. He won't talk about it, but I read through the file and something doesn't add up. I don't think he killed anyone, do you?"

"Well, no," I fumbled for words. "I've never thought he killed a soul, but he entered a guilty plea. Can you reopen a case that's closed like that?"

"Not officially, no," she admitted, "but I can do some digging and see what I turn up."

And, just like that, the lie that never ends cropped up yet again. I bit my tongue until I thought it would actually bleed.

"Does Eddie want you to do this?"

"I haven't asked him yet. I thought I would ask around and see what I come up with first."

"Patrice," I said finally, "I know you mean well, but I think you should ask Eddie if he wants you to do this before you go stirring up a pot that settled years ago."

"I'll ask him," she said.

"I *promise* I'll ask him," she repeated when she saw my dubious expression. "But, will you just tell me what you know about it? I know you had him to dinner that day; I remember spending Thanksgiving at your house and he was there. It was the day before Marcus died."

"I really just don't want to talk about it, hon," I said. "I'm sorry, but it was an awful time and we've all suffered enough."

"But if you could just..."

"Patrice!"

She flinched as if I'd slapped her.

"You ask Eddie first," I continued. "If he agrees, I'll tell you what I remember. Otherwise I think it's best that we let sleeping dogs lie."

"Okay," she said softly. "I meant no harm, but ... okay. I'll ask him first."

I knew she was upset that I yelled at her, and Lord knows she was confused, but I knew better than to even try to remember all the lies I told so many years ago.

"I've been thinking about my will," I said, abruptly changing the subject. "Do you do any estate law at all?"

"Goodness," she said. "No, I don't, but there are some great attorneys in the area if you want me to recommend someone."

"No, that's okay. Howard Hunnicutt has been handling our stuff for years. I'll just get him to dust the paperwork off and see where we are. I wonder, though..."

"Wonder what?" Patrice asked when I hesitated.

"If you would mind being the Executor of the estate." I finished.

"I don't mind at all. Anything you want to go over with me, so I'll be sure to get it right?"

"A few things, maybe," I said. "I'm not positive what I'm planning on doing, but I'd like to get your opinion on some ideas I have ... if you have time, that is."

Blanche interrupted then, bringing us each a glass of sweet tea and taking a seat in one of the rockers herself. She looked tired and drawn and I couldn't help but comment on it.

"You feeling all right, Blanche? You're looking a little peaked today."

"Just a little tired, tha's all. Ain't been sleepin' good lately."

"When's the last time you had a checkup?"

"I had my yearly," she said vaguely.

Blanche was not fond of doctors in general; though I had convinced her a few years back that she'd best take care of her health if she was going to be raising grandchildren from now on. I had enrolled Blanche and her family in our company health plan when I first went back to work. Don't ask why I hadn't done it when Walter was alive or why he hadn't suggested it, either. I just don't have an answer.

"That's not the kind of checkup I was talking about."

"I don't see the point. He's jus' go'n tell me to lose weight."

Well, I knew better than to go down that road, so I changed the subject fast.

We stayed on the porch for a little while longer, enjoying the cool breeze and watching the occasional passing car.

When Patrice and I finally sat down to discuss the will weeks later, I had formulated a plan of sorts. We talked at length about the details and, when we were done, I felt confident of the decisions I made.

Howard put me in touch with a good business broker and the insurance agency was sold within a month. I was surprised at the bottom line on the income from the sale, but Howard was not. We followed Walter's lead on a good bit of the estate planning, but we made a few changes. We increased the coffers of the scholarship fund quite a bit and set up another charitable remainder trust to offset the taxes on the sale.

What Patrice did *not* know about my will was that I planned to leave my house to Blanche for as long as she was alive. She probably spent as much time at this house as she had at her own, and I was certain it felt like home to her. After that, it would be sold and the proceeds sent to the scholarship fund, which Patrice had agreed to run after my death or when I could no longer handle my affairs. That was a huge load off my mind. Of course, she would now know how her own education had been funded, but I suspect she knew it all along anyway.

There was a monthly stipend earmarked for each of the twins. They were successful in their own right, but what I set out for them would make their lives a little more comfortable and it made me feel good to know that.

Grace's children would be able to attend the college of their choice. They were good kids, good students. I wanted to make sure nothing would stand in their way. Blanche would always have income, a retirement plan of sorts—enough for herself and enough to take care of Shawn and Rochelle.

As much as it tore my heart out, I did not leave anything for Grace. If we could even *find* her, the money would only go to drugs. I resigned myself to knowing we had already lost her. We lost her long, long ago and we were partially to blame.

Twenty Eight

As I said, 1998 was not a good year for me. My childhood friends were dropping like flies. I never expected to outlive as many people as I did, but if it's any indication how many funerals I attended, I bought four new dresses that year and all of them black. I've never been terribly vain, but I still held to a few social standards, even in my old age. I didn't want to be seen in the same black dress every time I turned around.

Poopsie died on a fishing trip out west. God love him, he went out with a bang, doing what he loved most. They had a time getting his body shipped home for burial, but Clara Jean handled all the details and got it straightened out. She was devastated, of course, and I'm not sure she's over it to this day.

The hardest thing for me, the worst day of my life, came in late November of that year. We had a lovely Thanksgiving dinner. Patrice and the twins cooked the entire meal in my kitchen and the house was brimming with food, friends, family and a whole lot of love. We all ate too much, but Blanche complained the most about it. She said she just felt full all over. Danita and Curtis drove her home afterwards, taking Shawn and Rochelle back to their own house to play with their cousins.

When Blanche didn't show up the next morning, I knew it was not good. I forced myself not to panic as I called a taxi to take me to her house. I decided not to call the children first. I didn't want to worry them in case I was wrong. On the other hand, if I was right ... well, if I was right, I would be the one who found her.

She didn't answer the door when I rang the bell, but I knew she never kept it locked. She always left it open, just in case Grace came home. I opened the door and entered the house, which had not changed much in the years since I came to take Patrice shopping. I could hear Blanche's snoring in the back bedroom and I breathed a sigh of relief. I figured she must have overslept, though she'd never done it before. I laughed at myself for overreacting and headed for her bedroom, scolding the whole way.

"Blanche, you old fool, you scared me to death!" I spoke loudly so I wouldn't startle her when I entered her room. "Blanche!" I repeated as I cleared the doorway. She was lying flat on her back, the covers kicked to the side and one arm hanging limply off the bed.

She didn't respond at all. She just laid there, air moving noisily in and out of her chest. I picked up her arm and shook it a little.

"Blanche, wake up," I said, shaking harder when she did not move. I think that's when I knew she was gone from me. I picked up the phone on her bedside table and dialed Patrice's number. I explained where I was and she said she would call the ambulance and be right over.

I didn't know what to do, so I did the first thing that came to mind. I went to the kitchen and put on a pot of water for tea. It seems ridiculous now, but that's what I did.

When I went back to Blanche's room, I carefully placed her hands on her stomach and pulled the blankets up to her chest. Then I crawled into the bed beside her, resting my head on her shoulder and one hand over both of hers. I watched my hand rise and fall with each breath, the sound rumbling in my ear.

I didn't move again until the ambulance arrived. I never heard the sirens. All I remember hearing was the sound of the teakettle screaming on the stove.

Patrice came in right behind them and we comforted each other as the paramedics tended to Blanche and hustled her into the ambulance. Patrice drove us to the hospital, calling her sisters from the cell phone.

Blanche lived another two weeks, though she never regained consciousness. In hindsight, I wish I'd never called a soul. I'd rather have just stayed right there until it was over, than to see my dear friend lying in a cold, sterile hospital room like that.

I've made up a new lie and I tell it to myself every day. Blanche died in her sleep, there in the house where she raised her children, amongst all her memories and all the things she loved. Marcus was there, and Grace, too. Grace, full of life and hope and promise. We were all there, me, Eddie, the twins—the whole family—there to tell Blanche goodbye and send her off to be with her husband again.

I've never been afraid of dying. I don't know what will happen when I do, but I have to believe I'll be with Walter again. I have to believe that I'll have another chance to tell him everything I did not know when he was on the earth and in my living room.

Twenty-nine

Grace did come home for the funeral, which went by in a blur for me. I remember so much about my life in those last twenty years, but I only barely recall being there for the service. The girls were inconsolable, I remember that. Blanche was 59 years old, far too young for the girls to be losing their mother to the stroke that ultimately took her life.

A week or so after the funeral, Patrice convinced Grace to get help for her drug addiction and, wouldn't you know, she started out at Lifeways downtown. She's been in and out of rehab ever since, though I heard she was doing well since her last relapse a few months ago. Patrice has been raising Grace's children for the most part, but Grace sees them often. She lives in Blanche's old house, which Patrice has fixed up quite a bit since her mother's death.

And now, here I am again. It is 2001 and I am preparing for yet another funeral. I'm too old for this, I've decided, and I'm never going to another funeral except my own after we bury The Pecan Man. I just can't do it anymore.

Chip Smallwood delivered Eddie's meager belongings to me a few days after he died alone in his cell. The tattered shoebox held a few small objects and several letters. There was a pewter lapel pin, wings with a bomb dead center. There were a few photographs, one of a very young Eddie in military uniform holding a girl no more than four or five years of age. Another of a smiling young woman in cap and gown. A note on the back read: *Dad, Sorry you couldn't be there with us. I know you're proud. Love, Tressa.*

The last was one I had taken the first Christmas Blanche and her girls spent with me. Gracie grinned from her perch on Eddie's lap. Blanche sat on the couch with one arm around Patrice and the twins at her feet. Chip and Clara Jean were squished together on the couch beside

Patrice. Chip was smiling awkwardly at the camera, but Clara Jean was looking up at him with the same adoration I had seen in the earlier pictures of Walter and me. The floor was littered with wrapping paper and shiny bows. It was a bittersweet time for all of us, and the photo made me a little sad.

The small stack of letters was tucked into an envelope embossed with Jeffery Thatcher's return address. There was Eddie's Last Will and Testament naming me as the Executor of his estate, such as it was, and a letter from Eddie addressed to me. He must have thought I'd live forever, or at least longer than he would. It was the first time I'd known for certain that he was not illiterate, as I'd often assumed. The writing was child-like but the spelling was good and I could read the words he wrote. I could tell he had put a lot of thought into what he wanted to say. There were two letters from Tressa Hightower, addressed to Eldred Mims in care of the prison, with a return address in Alabama.

The instructions for Eddie's burial were simple. Arrangements had already been made and his daughter had been called. I learned more about Eddie in the few days after his death than I had in the years preceding it. He was not quite as poor as I had expected, but was frugal with the meager income he did have. As such, he didn't wish to have his body sent to Alabama, but preferred the pauper's burial the state would provide, even if it meant that he would be laid to rest in a town that would forever remember his name with a mixture of horror and sadness, however wrongly imagined. The box came the day before Eddie's funeral and I made several phone calls to assure that he did not leave this world without a proper goodbye.

Thirty

Chip and Clara Jean Smallwood arrived the next day at 1:00 p.m. and took me to the graveside service out at the county cemetery. I recognized the chaplain from the prison. He had aged since the last time I saw him, but I remembered him as a kind man and one who genuinely cared about the souls of the inmates.

He was standing by the casket, speaking with a woman I had not met, but knew immediately. She was as dark as Blanche had been, but the opposite in stature. Tall and thin, Tressa Mims Hightower was an imposing figure, strikingly beautiful with sharp, intense features that did not immediately reflect the ready smile that greeted me when I introduced myself.

"Miz Beckworth, at last." Tressa's voice was as smooth as her mahogany skin.

"You're Eddie's daughter," I said.

"Yes, Ma'am. I'm Tressa Hightower."

"I have his belongings. He had two pictures of you, and a couple of others. Would you like to have them back?"

"Yes, Ma'am, I would. We don't have many photographs of my family in the early years."

I nodded. It was yet another thing I took for granted. I searched for something to say.

"Will you stay in Mayville for a while or are you leaving after the memorial?"

"I'll be leaving tomorrow morning. I have to stop in Montgomery before I head home."

"Business?" I asked.

"Always," she smiled. "I'm an attorney."

"Oh," I failed to keep the surprise from my voice. "Eddie didn't ...

Eddie never—"

"That's quite all right, Miz Beckworth." Tressa smiled again. "I didn't speak of him much either."

"I knew your father to be a good man," I said, suddenly a bit defensive.

"At times he was," she agreed. "I owe him a great deal."

"But?"

"Buts don't matter now, Miz Beckworth. It was what it was and it's over now. You're very kind and I appreciate what you tried to do for him. I know he appreciated it, too."

I didn't know how to respond to that. And it was not the time or place, regardless. I'd like to think it was kindness that I extended to Eddie, but I can't look back to a single thing I did for him that was selfless in any way.

A car pulled up beside us breaking the brief uncomfortable silence that had just taken hold. All four doors opened at once and Blanche's girls appeared, solemnly at first, but unable to disguise the smiles that were meant for me alone.

"Miz Ora!" Grace cried and bolted into my arms, causing Clara to clutch my elbow to support me.

Grace was rail-thin, almost emaciated. What frightened me the most was that Patrice told me how much better she looked now that she had been clean for a few months.

It was as if I were still holding that tiny broken child I took from Blanche's arms so many years ago. I wanted to go tuck her into bed and hide her wounds with soft chenille and a mother's sorrow.

"Let me look at you," I said and, forcing a smile, pushed her away from me and held her at arm's length.

"Miz Ora," she cried again, her tears flowing freely.

"Stop, or you'll make an old lady cry," I grumped.

"I'm sorry," she said. "It's just been so long."

"Too long," I agreed. "And who are these other women with you? My heavens, your sisters are getting old!"

Danita and ReNetta moved forward, each kissing me soundly on opposite cheeks. Patrice stood back, smiling like a mother with her brood. Blanche had been dead for only three years, but Patrice had always helped raise the other girls. It was Patrice who stayed in touch and kept me up to date with their lives. It was Patrice who continued to visit Eddie in prison when it became too difficult a journey for me to make. She saw him only two weeks before his death, took him a pound cake baked by Dovey Kincaid's daughter, who was now Patrice's best friend. The Lord works in mysterious ways, I've always thought.

Tressa Hightower cleared her throat behind me.

"Oh, goodness," I said. "I've forgotten my manners. Girls, there's someone I'd like you to meet."

I brought Tressa into my circle of family and made the necessary introductions. "These are Blanche's girls, Patrice, ReNetta, Danita and Grace. Girls, this is…" I hesitated only for a second. "This is your Aunt Tressa."

I'm not sure who was more stunned by my revelation. I hadn't intended to tell the girls until after the funeral. But, in that brief moment of introduction, truth compelled me like it never had before.

I explained, as briefly as I could, what Eddie's letter had revealed. We would talk more of it later, but for now it was only fitting and proper that the girls know for whom they were grieving and honor their grandfather for his life and for his sacrifice.

While everyone stood in open-mouthed silence, the chaplain called for the memorial to begin. The chaplain's words were kind, but rather generic, I thought. He spoke of Eddie's gentle nature, how he never caused trouble in his ward and how he was often called on to pray for others. He told of the pictures Eddie kept on his wall and how he must have truly loved and missed his family. He spoke of God's forgiveness and I felt comforted by that. By God's grace, I would one day be redeemed for my own shortcomings and that day had never seemed closer than it did when they lowered Eddie's body into the earth. I decided not to bury my lie with him, no matter what the cost.

And so now you have the complete and total truth. Bless Clara Jean's heart, she has sat and taken dictation for hours on end as I told my long and ragged tale. She has assured me her ears heard nothing that her mouth could ever tell, but her sure and able fingers would set down for me to disclose as I see fit.

Eldred Mims had not run away from his life in Alabama as much as he came home to his family in Mayville when he showed up here in 1975. When Blanche was born, Eddie left to join the new all-black Air Force in Tuskegee, Alabama. He said he always intended to come back, but time went by and he started a new life with another woman. Not wanting to make the same mistake, he married the mother of this child, the one they named Tressa.

I think Eddie really wanted to do the right thing, but addiction is sometimes stronger than the person it holds. And sometimes, like Eddie said, it's just too late to go back. I don't know why he never told Blanche, but I almost think she knew. My Lord, Blanche knew everything …

everything. Always.

I should have told Grace the truth after her mother died, but I didn't and there are more reasons why than I have time to tell. For now, Clara Jean is helping me pack. I don't know if I'll be going to jail or to a nursing home, but I can no longer live by myself regardless, so I'm going to one or the other.

I'm going to do the first selfless thing I've done in years. I'm giving my home to the girls, outright, free and clear. Well, not precisely free, but that's a tax issue that Howard worked out. But, they're paying only enough not to consider it a gift, but a purchase.

Patrice is handling the details of my confession. I didn't ask and I really don't want to know what the process will be. My goal is to clear Eddie's name and to admit what I did to help conceal who really killed Skipper Kornegay. As I said when I first began this story, I reckon there will be a few who wish I had kept my mouth shut. The ones who would truly be impacted are dead, though, and can surely rest in peace. As for me, I've not had a moment's peace since the day my first lie was told. I'm determined to go to my grave with a clear conscience, and I just can't do that until I tell the truth about Grace.

Maybe now, that precious girl can face her *real* demons and find her way in the world. I hope so. Lord knows I pray that she does.

About the Author

I was born and raised in Central Florida and, except for three formative years in Thomasville, Georgia and three more in Charlotte, NC where I met my true love and best friend, Perry Selleck, I have lived in Florida all my life. Sometime in the 90's my parents retired and moved to North Florida to escape the rapid (or maybe I should say rabid) growth that had made what I call my "hometown" nearly unrecognizable.

In 1998 Perry and I bought a piece of land on the Suwannee River that included a single-wide mobile home on stilts, intending to build a weekend home of sorts. Using chain saws and help from my brothers, we split that trailer into three parts, pushed it off its moorings and hauled it to the salvage yard. We spent nearly every weekend for the next three years driving to Mayo to work on our river house. Not long after it was livable, we decided we'd had enough of the growth ourselves and moved our family, which included our daughter Emily and our yappy little redhead Lucy, to the river. Thus began an adventure that almost immediately gave birth to the characters in The Pecan Man. (Note: the title word is pronounced Pee'-can)

One day in 2001, while coming back from the grocery store in Live Oak, I passed an old man riding a rumpled and rusted old bicycle down a narrow country road. Shortly after that, I passed a man picking up pecans in the front yard of his weathered old house. By the time I got home, I had the bones of my story and the three main characters, Ora Lee Beckworth, Blanche Lowery and Eldred Mims formed in my mind. Once I wrote the first chapter or two, the characters began to live and breathe and I allowed them to write the rest of their story. I make no apologies for my choice in writing the dialect as I hear the characters speak. These voices are as real to me as the characters themselves. And while they are all completely fictitious and are not intended to represent any real person, living or dead, I must admit that they all have characteristics of many people I have known.

The setting is the fictional town of Mayville, but some of the landmarks will be familiar to those in my hometown of Leesburg, Florida. Growing up in Central Florida during such a pivotal time in the Civil Rights era definitely influenced my perspective on the issue of race. I hope readers will forgive Ora her mistakes and celebrate her growth. She is a flawed character to be sure, as are we all.

CPSIA information can be obtained
at www.ICGtesting.com
Printed in the USA
FSOW03n2044210916
25257FS